To our first teachers:
Eugenia B. Nowicki
and
Eleanor O'B. Meehan

Interdisciplinary Strategies for English and Social Studies Classrooms

Interdisciplinary Strategies for English and Social Studies Classrooms

Toward Collaborative Middle and Secondary Teaching

JOSEPH JOHN NOWICKI

KERRY F. MEEHAN

Allyn and Bacon
Boston   London   Toronto   Sydney   Tokyo   Singapore

Copyright © 1997 by Allyn & Bacon
A Viacom Company
Needham Heights, MA 02194

Library of Congress Cataloging-in-Publication Data

Nowicki, Joseph John
    Interdisciplinary strategies for English and social studies
  classrooms : toward collaborative middle and secondary teaching /
  Joseph John Nowicki & Kerry F. Meehan.
      p. cm.
    Includes bibliographical references (p.   ) and index.
    ISBN 0-205-19839-2
    1. Language arts (Secondary)—United States.   2. Social sciences—
  Study and teaching (Secondary)—United States.
  3. Interdisciplinary approach in education—United States.
  I. Meehan, Kerry F.   II. Title.
  LB1631.N69   1997
  428′0071′2—dc20   96-1235
                                                          CIP

Printed in the United States of America
10 9 8 7 6 5 4 3 2 1   00 99 98 97 96

Contents

Preface

This is a book for middle, junior, and senior high school teachers and administrators, written to help educators meet the needs of students in changing schools. Through what we believe to be a teacher-friendly format, we suggest alternatives for educators to build schools that will provide the highest quality educational experiences for all students.

Specifically, the book presents nearly fifty interdisciplinary strategies to link social studies and English classes around common themes. We identify the common strengths gained by sharing areas of study while maintaining the unique character and integrity of English and social studies classes.

We believe this book is a marriage between the abstractions proposed by theorists and the realities practiced by teachers. In educational circles, theorists argue for implementation of their ideas into secondary classrooms. Teachers respond that they do not need more theory; they need practical advice and models for implementing better and more effective strategies. We have often heard the lament of teachers: "Great idea, but it won't work in my class," or "Those ideas are too general. How do we put them to work?" or the opposite side of the frustration: "That is too specific. No way can I use that with my kids."

This book meets the need to translate theory into action. It does not preach at teachers to abandon current practices, but offers a continuum of student-centered interdisciplinary strategies, lasting from one day to a term, which are grounded in the latest educational research. A number of the strategies that appear in this book are the products of over forty accumulated years of teaching English and social studies. Others are hybrids that we see as models for meeting the needs of interdisciplinary and collaborative classrooms. This book is a blend of strategies for traditional teachers, as well as those who practice a more experimental approach.

Our approach is to arrange strategies categorically for thematic interdisciplinary activities and teaching. The first group of strategies is designed to last from a day to a few weeks, followed by more comprehensive activities created for term-long units and various ideas for year-long interdisciplinary and thematic work. We include a rationale for each theme as well as suggested lessons and classroom activities for the short-term and unit-length themes. Each lesson identifies subject-specific factual, conceptual, and skill-based material. Also included are common objectives for establishing student expectations, outcomes, and specific strategies for assessment.

Both of us are veteran teachers who view schools as vibrant places filled with enormous potential. We share a belief in the importance of creating classrooms that utilize mixed ability groupings and represent the diversity of a school community. Our backgrounds include work in both tracked and mixed-ability social studies and English classrooms.

Additionally, we have experiences as a special-needs teacher and graduate-level educator in administration and curriculum (Joe) and as an administrator (Kerry). We also share with teachers the frustration of trying to implement change. We further understand that teachers and administrators trying to implement change can be overwhelmed by theory that is not translated into practical terms reflecting the daily realities of school life. This book exemplifies what can happen when two teachers come together to share and build on their ideas.

As teachers, we have dealt with implementing change in our classrooms and through our work as educational consultants. We see the need and strength of creating collaborative classrooms in which students work together. We see an even greater need to enable teachers to do the same. Both students and teachers must have the opportunity to be directly involved in what is learned and taught. To achieve this goal, we present practical strategies that unite teacher with teacher and students with students in common and shared activities for the enhancement of teaching and learning. What we suggest contributes to a process that enables members of a school community to gain greater control over their lives.

The introductory chapter of this book emphasizes the need to make schools more collaborative. Drawing on educational and sociological literature, this first chapter addresses the ways traditional models for organizing schools tracked students and teachers while stifling the creative potential that flows from collaborative involvement. Ways of creating and strengthening heterogeneous classrooms through interdisciplinary activities are explored. The chapter concludes with a statement of the need to utilize the diversity brought to classrooms by all learners.

A second chapter offers suggestions for helping teachers create interdisciplinary situations. The chapter includes a description of how schools create barriers between teachers, isolating them from each other. It highlights a number of the pitfalls educators may face and offers some alternative paths to follow.

Chapters 3, 4, and 5 contain strategies for creating interdisciplinary activities based on themes that highlight the strengths and diversity of mixed-ability classrooms. Chapter 3 includes more than forty examples of interdisciplinary work. Chapter 4 presents six complete units. Chapter 5 describes methods to incorporate themes to be studied not only into social studies and English classes, but into the whole life of the school.

We also confront issues that teachers and administrators encounter in dealing with change. Our strategies are flexible; we expect teachers to modify what we offer to fit their specific needs and the needs of their students. We also see this work applying to a varied cross-section of teachers. Some of our models address the needs of teachers who are beginning a dialogue in hopes of finding ways to share what they do. Other thematic activities are more complex and utilize unit-length themes based on a team teaching approach.

Often we found ourselves writing in the voice of an English teacher, a social studies teacher, a special-needs teacher, or an administrator. At other times, we found ourselves expressing the frustrations we have shared as teachers interested in creating interdisciplinary connections for our students. As the frustration grew within us, while creating strategies that crossed discipline lines, we recognized that, indeed, social studies and English teachers, particularly in traditional settings, hold very different perspectives of what they do. Choices about what should be taught and how it should be taught truly reflect the primacy that each group feels. At this point, we recognized that the need for learning must transcend disciplines and that compromise is essential. Once we recognized this, our brainstorming and reflection about identifying commonalities in English and social studies classes bordered on celebrating a profession.

Although we base our interdisciplinary work on linking social studies and English classes around common themes, we do not mean to exclude other subject areas. In fact, we see our models leading directly to assimilate any number of disciplines in common activities.

Our focus in this work, which reflects our shared vision of what schools can be, is threefold. It focuses first on collaboration between teachers, second on the collaboration necessary among students, and third on breaking down the isolation of content areas. We suggest both beginning and alternative paths to follow. Our commitment is to reaffirm that quality education can be provided to all students in collaborative settings by capitalizing on the shared strengths of students and teachers.

Finally, a note about the voices of both teachers and students that appear throughout the book. These quotations were generated in the process of researching the impact of heterogeneous grouping and school change on teachers and students for earlier educational reports.

ACKNOWLEDGMENTS

We wish to thank the following reviewers for their helpful suggestions: Bonnie M. Smith, Hettinger High School, North Dakota, and Shirley A. Rau, Nampa High School, Idaho.

Interdisciplinary Strategies for English and Social Studies Classrooms

CHAPTER 1

Introduction

> *"Working together with other kids makes me feel real close to my teachers."*
>
> "Tom"

We see this book as a guide for building bridges and connecting people. We offer ways to encourage students to work with other students, teachers to work with other teachers, and administrators to support each of these groups. The models we have designed and highlighted in this book are the beginning of bridging the gap that all too often exists between educational theory and classroom practice.

Interdisciplinary Strategies for English and Social Studies Classrooms: Toward Collaborative Middle and Secondary Teaching is aimed primarily at middle, junior high, and high school English and social studies teachers. The label *social studies* also includes various related subject areas—history, geography, law, and a number of other social sciences. Beyond that, we see our audience including all middle, junior high, and senior high school teachers, administrators, and building, city, and districtwide supervisors who create and establish policy for schools. Likewise, when we use the term *heterogeneous grouping,* we affirm our earlier working definition that heterogeneous grouping, nontracked or heterogeneous classrooms, are those that "are *not* grouped by gender, socio-economic, or ethnic background, culture, or ability" (Nowicki & Meehan, 1996, p. vi).

Classrooms in many secondary schools represent models for organization that have been followed for approximately a half century. Granted, there has been movement toward embracing innovation in elementary schools, and change has continued to creep into junior high and middle schools, but senior high schools, for the most part, remain organized as they have been for many decades. Schools are differentiated by department and organized according to classrooms. Students go through a daily schedule punctuated by bells; they take classes that fall along a subject-area sequence indicated by departmental policy, school requirements, and state regulations. Students choose elective courses that, fitted neatly into a schedule, offer some diversion from the prescribed and ordered routines of school life. These electives, however, also are arranged from a departmental perspective rather than one dealing with schoolwide or student-centered concerns.

A school organizes teachers' lives just as it organizes students'. High school teachers still live within the realm of their departments and subject areas. They are involved with schoolwide committees and many extracurricular issues that represent the totality of life in a high school, but the way many high school teachers conduct their professional lives and carry out their craft remains ordered and organized along departmental lines. This is particularly true of schools that maintain rigid tracks in the way students are grouped. Departmental differences alone are enough to isolate many students and educators. The added burden of tracks solidifies the detachment that many students and teachers feel about their work.

Educational reform has taken center stage over the past decade in educational literature. Teachers, administrators, and boards of education are urged to rethink and redirect their energies as they reinvent their schools. Researchers, policymakers, and theorists enliven the debate with a stream of recommendations for schools to follow, such as the need to bring heterogeneity to classrooms. The emphasis on change in schools is enough to leave many classroom educators reeling. Often, issues lumped together under the reform rubric constitute little more than ideas for the practicing education professional who spends day after day working in the classroom.

In our experience, many educators are interested in issues of reform. Despite the additional hours of work such a commitment adds to an already overtaxed schedule, many teachers are willing to adapt change to their classrooms and to their schools. What teachers tell us they need are models they can use to bring ideas espoused by reformers into practice, models that must be flexible enough to be modified for the needs of an educator in any school.

As teachers, struggling ourselves with change, we understand these voices. We recognize the need to reorganize and have experienced the ensuing frustrations of making changes within the rigid structure of some high schools. We understand the hesitation of colleagues who have wished reform efforts to go further in *their* school. Our experience has included our own share of frustration and failure as well as success, but we have also *learned* from our experiences. *Strategies* presents a model for building interdisciplinary learning units in inclusive schools and is based on our introductory work (Nowicki & Meehan, 1996) dealing with lessons that use *facts, concepts,* and *skills* as components for student success. The models that we offer respect our belief in the importance of heterogeneity in classrooms. As teachers, we write for practicing and potential teachers; additionally, we hope this book may help break down some of the barriers that hinder the initiation of reform efforts.

THE FORCE FOR REDEFINING CLASSROOMS IN A CHANGING WORLD

"When I went to another school, it wasn't heterogeneous. It was four different groups and it was top group got the green book, next group got the orange book, next group got the blue book . . . you know what I mean. It was obvious, everybody knew who was in the top class and who wasn't. I don't think people tried half as hard as they do here."

"Mary"

The world, simply put, is not the same place it was fifty years ago. Yet we need only look at the past (Waller, 1932) to see how very similar our present-day schools are to those of an earlier era. Unfortunately, beliefs such as homogeneous grouping of students (Oakes, 1985) stem from a model developed during the educational debate that took place around the turn of the century. Placing students in tracks or predetermined groups reflecting ability level only facilitated the departmentalization of high schools and contributed toward fostering inequality within those schools (Oakes, 1985; Bowles & Gintis, 1976). The direction was toward efficiency because of the numbers of students who were entering schools during the early part of the century. Oakes states that "between 1890 and 1918 an average of more than one new high school was built for each day" (Oakes, 1985, p. 19), and the emphasis was also on arranging students according to certain criteria. As a result, students were often separated from other students and teachers from other teachers.

Schools at that time faced a dilemma—an enormous influx of students, representing a diverse range of ethnic communities in which English was not the primary language. The response was to build larger and larger schools. These larger organizations were seen as needing a structure that would keep them efficient. This need for an expertly driven organization in which units functioned as contributors to the whole was resolved in the work of the German sociologist Max Weber. Writing in the early 1900s, Weber proposed a model of bureaucracy (Weber, 1946, 1947, 1956) that offered organizations a rational alternative for self-organization and efficient governance.

Educators in the United States, confronted with the growing student populations in the infancy of public education, opted for this bureaucratic model. Schools were organzed in what was seen then as the most rational way possible. The birth of tracking and departmentalization went hand in hand with the building of large schools designed to meet the particular needs of a growing and diverse audience. At the time, education was responding to the cries from an industrial base that needed behaviorally compliant workers rather than intellectual innovators (see, e.g., Bowles & Gintis, 1976).

Teachers are still dealing with this legacy of the past. Educators still rely on a bureaucratic departmentalization of schools, which systematically tracks students. These same tracks organize teachers, too. Both teachers and students are kept apart from colleagues and peers by the structure of the schools in which they live and work. The system that organizes educators and students may well be one of the factors blocking educational and professional growth. There is significant evidence from the literature (e.g., Lieberman, 1988; Lieberman & Miller, 1991; Goodlad, 1984) suggesting that it is pertinent for educators to question their faith in the way that schools persist in being organized, a manner that divides people rather than bringing them together to share work for common goals.

The United States is part of a world society, and diversity within U.S. society is a reality. Futurists predict that the culture will adjust itself to basic population changes. Industry demands that we find a way to graduate students who are or can become technically able. Our democratic form of government demands that we have an educated populace to deal with the ever-increasing demands of the future. Models of schooling devised at the turn of the century simply will not work any more.

Since 1956, the U.S. economy has had a larger percentage of the population employed in service than in manufacturing. Yet our schools have failed to recognize the consequent change in the type of education that needs to be provided. The computer revolution has further altered the demands of education, both economically and socially, yet again schools have been slow to respond to societal changes. We cannot rely on schools and classrooms that continue to separate and build barriers against linking students and educators in collaborative learning and a collaborative society.

THE CONCEPT OF WORKING TOGETHER: TEACHERS

One of the recent themes of educational reform has centered on enabling teachers to work together. Before teachers can expect students to work together in collaborative classrooms, they first need to expect the same from fellow teachers. It is the teachers who model the efforts of collaborative work for students. As teachers, we feel that this recognition about professional practice has been long overdue. Modeling this principle is the work of two teachers working together to create this book. Our earlier work (Nowicki & Meehan, 1996) on collaborative social studies classrooms was another model of this activity and the positive results of teacher-sharing.

Bringing teachers together to share their work and their ideas about learning has been a recent ideal in education. Again, the professional literature is replete with work dedicated to allowing teachers the opportunity to share their work—for example, Bolman and Deal (1994), Barth (1990), and Nowicki (1992). We understand that teachers are often separated and compartmentalized in much the same way as tracked students. We share a social studies assignment and jointly decide what we would like to do with our classes (although we continue to teach separate grade levels and are part of two separate departments). Both of us have past experience working with teachers at different schools and outside of our disciplines to build shared curricula. More often than not, systemic organization stymied such efforts and shunted us back to the realms of classroom, subject, and department; yet we have learned lessons that are valuable to all teachers interested in professional collaboration and to administrators interested in reorganizing their schools. The first is that teachers working at specific grade levels can work in *teams,* as opposed to working as interdisciplinary *team teachers.* Ultimately, the first designation leads to the second.

Teaming

> *"I like it the best when we've done things in classes that had teachers from different subjects working together."*
>
> "Al"

We define *teaming* as teachers serving students in populations at similar age levels, sharing insights that foster student success and developing a plan in which skill-based areas, common to the needs of the student population, can be addressed. Our definition allows for teachers to work together both across and within disciplines. Evidence exists (e.g., Wheelock, 1992) that supports the practice and concept of teachers striving toward a common purpose.

While teaming fosters the sense of working together so often lacking in departmentalized and tracked schools, it also enables educational professionals to develop goals for the same set of students. When we have worked as members of *teams,* whether within departments or across the curriculum, our efforts at collaboration have rewarded our students with understanding a concise set of expectations reinforced by common teachers.

At the basic level, teaming offers teachers a chance—and that is just what it is—to talk together about what they do. Conversations, our experience tells us, lead to common concerns about what students need and what should be addressed by grade-level curriculum.

At a more advanced level, teaming offers teachers the opportunity to develop a set of skills that can be measured. Learning skills, important to all future academic success, are the essence of what teachers consider their focus. These skills are not grounded in curriculum but are linked to expectations for students at a certain age level. Developing these skills offers the school and the community the opportunity to decide directly what skills should be met at specific grade levels. Furthermore, heterogeneity in classrooms demands that skills occupy a primary point in assessing students' progress and development. The result will be greater student involvement in the direction of their own acquisition of knowledge as they work toward mastery of certain skills.

Teaming of teachers across a grade level also enables teachers to develop collaborative themes that move beyond skill levels, but to translate those skills into application in content areas. The focus of this work represents the result of working together, of sharing high points, and of commiserating about difficulties.

In our definition, born through practice, teaming should lead to team teaching as content areas begin to be complemented by the collaborative work of teachers of students at similar age levels. Teaming gives teachers the opportunity to *learn* to work together and to develop common agreements regarding students' mastery of skills. Experience tells us that teachers, particularly at the high school level, have learned to teach as individuals working within a particular classroom and with a dedicated subject matter. Individualism is important to teaching, but it is also a barrier that keeps teachers from working with one another. For example, the issue of evaluation can be a point of contention. Two teachers working together are, in a sense, outside of traditional departmental parameters at the high school. Which department's rubric will be selected for assessment? Who will evaluate their work? Which department holds jurisdiction? How and to what degree is their work interconnected? Finally, how do such endeavors affect the provisions of the school system or regional contract? There are no hard and fast answers to these questions, particularly when they are asked of teachers operating in rigidly structured schools organized according to an inflexible bureaucratic model.

There are some solutions, however. One, in particular, means modifying the bureaucratic models found in schools, models that control teachers' professional lives by prohibiting them from forming a collegial dialogue with peers. Volumes of professional literature extol the benefits of teachers working together, but also the numbers of collaborative works written by the rank and file teachers seem to support the current practices enforcing isolation.

Often, talk of changing teachers' organization elicits fear from the very people the innovation is aimed at helping. Many teachers have assumed a defensive posture. Teaching has become increasingly complex, with many more demands placed on teachers both from within and from outside the profession. Many of those demands stem from calls for change that would radically alter the way many teachers practice their craft. In addition, a constant stream of criticism is aimed at teachers by policymakers and those who represent taxpayers. It is no wonder that teachers react defensively to proposals for restructuring relationships within schools.

Nevertheless, changing or modifying a model to enable teachers to work together within and across disciplines in a team dedicated to a common theme at the high school level offers many benefits. As practitioners, we have found that teaming according to grade levels and developing teacher-generated themes contributes to teachers' growth and professional development. For example, for teachers dealing with bureaucratic change, teaming offers the security of remaining autonomous within a classroom where teachers are most comfortable with subject matter and teaching styles. At the same time, it offers the sense of collaborative support so lacking in the teaching profession today.

> *"I see a whole lot of people more involved, more professional. Heterogeneous grouping has forced cooperation among all staff members and all departments within the school."*
>
> Mr. "T"

At its highest point, teaming allows teachers the collaborative time to recognize common skill-based and content-based themes. From our own participation in the experience, we feel that teachers working together not only provide model behavior for the heterogeneous classroom, but also contribute a more collaborative and cooperative element to the faculty and culture within a school.

WORKING TOGETHER: STUDENTS

> *"Working together makes it easier for kids in our school who are slower than others because it is better for them and the ones that excel in the classroom. It's challenging them to learn. We push each other."*
>
> "Molly"

We will not offer a defense of the concept of students working together in a collaborative way. The professional literature suggests that collaboration and cooperative learning empower students toward success (Wheelock, 1992). Our experience agrees with these assessments, particularly within heterogeneous classrooms. Collaboration within cooperative classrooms benefits all students.

Teachers working collaboratively connect students with each other and with the content in their school lives. A school day that organizes six or seven hours into seven or eight periods isolates students within a particular learning context. All too often, the interconnections that should be the staple and celebration of school life are ignored in favor of a bureaucratically arranged structure that denies students access to the interconnectedness essential to intellectual and social growth.

Not only are students separated into classrooms drawn along subject area lines; they also may be arranged within subject areas by tracks or leveled groups. These divisions only further separate students from each other and create divisions within a school. In a sense, students separated from each other in the context of a school day represent the power of a bureaucratic model over the needs of the individual. As the model keeps teachers from teachers and slows interdisciplinary professional growth, it also inhibits students from gaining access to the full experience of their schooling. Sorting students into isolated departments and then tracking them within those departments denies unlimited opportunity for intellectual and social growth. Furthermore, it violates the idea of educating students for membership in a truly democratic society. One way of bringing students together while also meeting the separate and equally important needs of teachers is through developing material that can be used directly by teachers and students in schools.

THE DEVELOPMENTAL NATURE OF THEMES: STEPS TO FOLLOW

Does our model guarantee success? No. Schools are interpersonal places, where organizational culture plays a major role (Brubaker, Case, & Reagan, 1994; Bolman & Deal, 1991; Rossman, Corbett, & Firestone, 1988). Recognizing the politics involved in the decision-making process, we can easily see the difficulty of bringing any new model to a school. Despite these obstacles, we feel there are alternatives in bringing high school teachers to the initiating step of working together.

We are teachers from two distinct backgrounds. Kerry is a veteran English teacher who has also developed an affinity for teaching social studies. Joe is a veteran social studies teacher who has taught English. While Joe also brings the experience of special education to his work, Kerry brings an understanding of the difficulties of a teacher's life gained through his administrative tenure as an assistant principal. Our combined experience tells us that there is a need for linking teachers at the junior high and high school and that there are also valid and viable ways of doing this.

We feel that *themes can provide a primary link to the experience and professional practice of teachers in junior and senior high schools.* Themes offer subject-area teachers the opportunity to link skills, the fact-based learning, and their students' conceptual discoveries with those of their colleagues. Themes also serve as building blocks in a progression from simple steps to more complex tasks. For example, skill-based themes that are age- or grade-centered can run through a curriculum shared by many teachers rather than focusing the work of many individual teachers, with skills running the gamut from those at a basic or introductory level to those that represent mastery of higher level thinking.

The same can be said for concept mastery. In both cases, teachers can share lines of thought that are clear-cut and that tie disciplines and classrooms together rather than separate them and hold them apart. Teachers are linked by the commonality of the knowledge they bring to the classroom, which is grounded in the curriculum they have created and teach.

Themes offer opportunities for English and social studies teachers to build on commonalities inherent in teaching across the curriculum focused on an age level. Themes present a clear-cut progression of learning skills and concepts, from lower to higher order complexity.

WHAT IS COMMON IN THE CURRICULUM? WHAT IS NOT?

> *"It is frustrating for me as a teacher to think that another teacher is covering similar ideas as I am, but we never get the chance to share what we're doing."*
>
> Ms. "P"

Let's envision an English teacher and a social studies teacher studying each other's course content. Both teach ninth graders. We would not be surprised to see them find many similarities in what they were teaching. Both stress affective skills necessary for success in the classroom and in life. To their students, these skills focus on behaviors such as organizing, working cooperatively, being punctual and reflecting on attitudes in such issues as in a growing sense of responsibility among students. Other skills observed in both curricula that focus directly on what takes place in the classroom are conducting research, interviewing, developing a writing style, or breaking down text for understanding and interpretation, among others.

A closer look at the curricula from the two classes leads us to see common concepts that come from any study or representation of human experience. These concepts, such as the struggle between life and death or the constant shift between social order and chaos, are the essentials of human experience, shared by those studying literature or history. Diverse conceptual frameworks manifest themselves in any English or social studies curriculum because they are the *stuff* of our existence as human beings.

Our seasoning as educators tells us that what is common in both curricula is highlighted even more in classrooms where students are organized heterogeneously rather than in rigid and arbitrary groups based on some predetermined level of ability. In nontracked classrooms, as our previous work (Nowicki & Meehan, 1996) indicates, learning skills and conceptual understandings receive more attention than in classrooms that are rigidly tracked. Linking teachers by what is common in their teaching brings students together in the commonness of their learning.

So far, we have considered the commonalities shared by English teachers and social studies teachers rather than the separate and distinct course content involved. The factual material covered in a particular social studies class or English class is unique. Too often, in traditionally tracked classrooms, a dependence on factual material drives the curriculum, rather than an equal recognition of the importance of skill-based learning or of developing conceptual understandings (see, e.g., Nowicki & Meehan, 1996, for a further discussion of this point). Looking at a ninth-grade English and social studies curriculum, we would conclude that there were differences in the material being taught and in the factual knowledge unique to each.

Likewise, our investigation would lead us to recognize a difference in the perspectives of each teacher as evidenced in the curriculum. We borrow the term *perspective* (Charon, 1989; Shibutani, 1955; Rossman et al., 1988; Corbett, Firestone, & Rossman, 1987; Bolman & Deal, 1988; Nowicki, 1992, 1994) as it is used in both educational and sociological research, where sociologists Becker, Geer, Hughes, and Strauss define it as

> a coordinated set of ideas and actions a person uses in dealing with some problematic situation, to refer to a person's ordinary way of thinking and feeling about and acting in such a situation. These thoughts and actions are co-ordinated in the sense that the actions flow reasonably, from the actor's point of view, from the ideas contained in the perspective. Similarly, the ideas can be seen by an observer to be one of the underlying rationale for the person's actions and are seen by the actor as providing a justification for acting as he does. (1984, p. 34)

There are clear, recognizable perspectives that define what it means to be an English teacher or a social studies teacher. Those self-definitions come from separate knowledge bases and from a history that for many years has stressed independence rather than interdependence in curriculum and teaching. This is but another example of the effects of rigid bureaucratic structures in many schools, which have compartmentalized teachers rather than freed them up to take advantage of their professional diversity.

Each teacher's perspectives are rooted in the factual material that traditionally has driven the curriculum. Once the curriculum is opened up and focuses on other issues, such as interrelated skills and concepts, the isolation born of perspectives grounded in one style of subject matter begins to give way.

Finally, we should make it clear that we do not see the existence of distinct perspectives as having only a negative effect on teachers and students. There is an important benefit in recognizing the underlying rationale and orientation that each subject area teacher brings to the art and science of teaching. Understanding the perspectives of another and being willing to borrow as well as to compromise while *maintaining* their *sense of disciplinary integrity* benefits both teachers and their students.

PROTECTING TURF

A common obstacle to teachers working within rigidly structured schools, in which the differences in course content reflect a divided and often competing set of perspectives, is the notion that finding common ground results in a loss of course content. In this case, course content is seen as representing "professional turf." Both sides in our example, represented by the English teacher and the social studies teacher and their specific curricula, may feel that they have a mission to be on guard and to protect what is theirs. It is not surprising that this mode of thinking governs interactions between teachers in schools that have a rigid organizational and social structure. Rigidly bureaucratic schools based on strictly departmental lines force teachers to feel separate and to hold onto what is theirs as if knowledge were a material possession that was deeded to certain individuals because of their title of "English teacher" or "social studies teacher."

In our experience, it is important to recognize and respect the perspectives of various teachers and to use their viewpoints for common professional growth. It is also important to understand some of the common concerns expressed by teachers when they face the issue of cross-disciplinary work.

Concerns from the English Teacher

> *"No way am I giving up teaching Shakespeare!!"*
> Mr. "M"

What am I going to give up? What am I going to lose? How much of my teaching am I to change? These are questions commonly asked by both English and social studies teachers facing collaborative assignments. The questions are valid and need to be addressed.

In planning the curriculum work for a ninth- or tenth-grade English class, teachers need to consider a number of issues. The two primary concerns of the English teacher are developing effective writers and comprehensive readers. A further glance at a scope and sequence for the grade, although it may vary a bit from school to school because of the involvement of process writing, reader responses to literature, journaling, and whole language, will still include subunits and mini-lessons on figures of speech, on writing patterns such as comparison, contrast, exposition, and so on. The literature may call for units on the short story, poetry, drama, nonfiction, the novel, and on and on. Questions such as "Why is there not enough time in the year to complete this task?" and "How can I give up some of my time to work on supporting social studies?" bombard the theory of change and can lead to stasis.

Additionally, many of these areas are subject-specific. Among these are recognizing and creating figures of speech such as similes and metaphors; the use of personification, symbols, irony, and satire; and establishing point of view and tone in, for example, a Shakespearean play or a novel by Robert Cormier.

Although not governed as social studies teachers are by the need to reach a certain date in history or to "cover" a world war before summer vacation, English teachers feel more bound by the need to complete tasks and skill-oriented functions. Many of these skills are taught through thematic units—courage, love, coming of age, humans and their environment. Through a marriage of theme and skills, English teachers will increase students' interest and put skills into a wider context.

At this point, the issues of commonality start to become clear. Is what we do really so very different? The rigidity of tracked classrooms bound to a prescribed curriculum implies that English and social studies are different from each other. Yet a closer examination of the lesson or unit from a basis of identifying the *facts, skills,* and *conceptual learning* is revealing.

On a factual level, there may be a wide disparity between the two areas. Metaphors, nouns, sentence construction, and spelling rules are different types of facts than 1066, the Treaty of Versailles, Martin Luther, the feudal system, or the Holocaust. As one moves to the level of skill development, however, commonalities become much clearer. Issues such as primary research, note taking, creating a formal essay, using documentation, following a line of reasoning to argue a point, and constructing thesis statements are skills that often are taught in both areas and, at times, with confusing particulars based on the biases of the two teachers.

> *"I knew I could teach in a heterogeneous classroom when I realized that I didn't have to teach* Ivanhoe."
>
> Ms. "N"

Consequently, the area most important for each discipline is also the area in which discussion and compromise must occur for interdisciplinary activities to succeed. That is in the area of themes, which lead to the conceptual development of knowledge. Whereas English looks at individual human themes such as coming of age, social studies tends to look at more societally based themes, such as order versus chaos, or nationalism. Yet there are bridges to deal with these differences. Novels such as Cynthia Rylant's *Castles I Have Seen* (1993) or Hemingway's *A Farewell to Arms* (1929), contain both individual themes and historical content. With mutual respect and a spirit of compromise for the greater benefit of the students, interdisciplinary work can succeed.

It is also important to examine the nature of Language Arts as a discipline. In our experience, language arts is the strength that drives the curriculum in many ways. The art and culture of a time are reflected in the literature of the period. History is the events, the people, and the actions of the society. Literature is the record of the times told through novel, drama, short story, poetry, journal, art, and music. In many ways, language arts really is a study of the arts. Literature is an emotional reflection from art, music, and dance as creators attempt to discover the truth and pass it on to future generations. English, as it is still called in secondary curricula, is the discipline that gains its strength through the very nature of being supportive to the other liberal arts. Its particular strength comes from its adaptability to supporting other disciplines while retaining its unique character through literature. Yet in schools, we have altered that strength as a support for the other disciplines and have attempted to change the special character of English. The complexity and universality of literature come from its ability to record in varied genres humanity's quest for truth. The skill levels of language arts should be shared with other departments to enable students to compete in a literate world and in a global society that demands thinking skills of the highest order.

These are the real issues that must be addressed for collaboration to occur; therefore, it is necessary to examine the way this theory of interdisciplinary units will benefit English and/or language arts. For this unit, a ninth-grade class will be the age/grade-level group: What is the general scope and sequence for the ninth grade? This varies widely, but generally it is the year in which students begin to build literary skills by working specifically with the various genres of literature, short story and novel, poetry and drama, and forms of nonfiction. Additionally, students at this grade level are usually working on writing skills, including parts of speech and sentence and paragraph structures, as well as practicing forms of writing to develop characterization, persuasion, theme, comparison and contrast, point of view, and a voice and style of their own. Underscoring these skill development areas are skills in vocabulary and word attack, listening and speaking, reading and thinking. At this point, examine closely what is coming into focus. All issues above are *skill-developing* areas of expertise. English, especially on the ninth-grade level, is primarily a skill-based curriculum.

Many of the skills enumerated here are equally important in other areas within the school. Are students taught English for the sake of knowing English, or are they taught language arts for the purpose of entering into other areas with a common ground of language, written and oral, and reading and thinking skills that will allow them to decode other texts, complete assignments, and develop higher order thinking? Language arts is not an end product; it is a set of skills that provide literature, human discourse, and common vocabulary for communication. With these ideas in mind, is English giving anything up to social studies? No. Both disciplines benefit from sharing the responsibilities of instruction and reinforcement.

Following skills, a major component of any English class is literature, the heart and soul of language arts and the raison d'être for many high school English teachers. A love of the written word and the quest for truth has turned many undergraduates into English majors. To understand English teachers, look at the selection of authors and works that make up the syllabus. It is through the *selection* of the literature that English teachers personalize a course and unconsciously illustrate bias. English teachers who have created this domain may not want to share or jeopardize it. This is their turf, in the strongest meaning of the word.

However, compromise is necessary in the creation of the interdisciplinary unit. The English teachers do not relinquish the literature component of the course but are responsible for selecting the appropriate reading material for interdisciplinary education to work. Some of these new selections may not be their personal favorites, but that is the compromise needed in interdisciplinary teaching. This approach may necessitate a wider range of materials or changes in methodology, which we will demonstrate as the unit unfolds. English teachers should realize that, in relinquishing certain titles, they are gaining allies in the form of the social studies teachers to help introduce, teach, and reinforce other critical skills that are the foundation for reading and writing, no matter the discipline.

A related issue in interdisciplinary work is the time allotted to teaching specific skills. Many minutes and even periods are expended in stressing, reviewing, and reinforcing selected skills. Why does this take so much time? Why don't students remember the material and show dexterity with the skill immediately? Why is there so much regression in the course of their progression? One answer is related to the isolation of teachers, classes, and course content from the full picture of students' learning. If certain reading, writing, thinking, and presenting skills are stressed only in one class, students will not generalize this information but will keep it in a mental "locker" to be opened only in that class. When teachers work in an interdisciplinary and teaming style, students receive the information from more than one source. Consequently, stronger imprinting occurs and less time is needed in each class to repeat and remediate. The end result is more time to reach the conceptual levels that are the product of effective instruction.

Concerns from the Social Studies Teacher

"Themes are wonderful, but what do I do about state achievement tests?"

Mr. "D"

Social studies teachers, like all educators, must address many issues in planning and carrying out their teaching. For example, consider the demands on a ninth-grade social studies' teacher. A traditional class may use a text mandated by a school, a district, or even a state. Teachers must teach a myriad of facts about a distant time, including facts about events, dates, and geography. Social studies teachers must make the material interesting and involving for current ninth graders. Along with teaching this body of factual material, teachers are also required to teach a body of skill-based material—understanding charts, reading maps and graphs, and creating time lines—specific to the subject area. Additionally, social studies teachers must create situations and present material that will allow and stimulate students to arrive at conceptual understandings of the issues that are critical to learning.

At this point, the school administration, tracking, and teacher isolation become major factors affecting teacher performance, accountability, and turf. Tight bureaucratic control over teachers' professional lives creates increased pressure on teachers to meet the needs of the curriculum. The result is a rigidly structured class. Rather than serving the teachers' and students' needs, the curriculum reinforces the traditional administrative hierarchy.

Furthermore, our experience supports our belief that the more a social studies class is tracked, the more teachers and students must meet the demands of a fact-driven curriculum. Our best example is our own fear of running out of time and not bringing a course to closure. Consequently, our students remain limited in their knowledge and in their development of a personal sense of historical reality.

This is not to say that content can be separated from what social studies teachers do. It cannot. Social studies teachers are responsible for covering a specific and explicit body of factual knowledge that is unique to the discipline. This is particularly true when one considers the multitude of history-based courses taught in our schools. The concerns of these teachers, in a discussion of interdisciplinary issues, often revolve around the amount of material to be covered. In addition, their concerns focus on specific skill issues, such as connecting fact-based historic and geographic understandings. True, these skill-based concerns can be overemphasized at times. Is it imperative to teach about the Congress of Vienna in a world history course lasting one year and running from the creation of the world to the present day? Such arcane questions are issues that social studies teachers face every year.

For an effective sense of interdisciplinary action to take place in schools, both social studies and English teachers must recognize the unique needs of each discipline and compromise in some areas while maintaining key learnings of particular importance (strategies in subsequent chapters offer examples of such compromises). In a sense, the two groups of teachers, working together, need to reach a working accommodation *respecting* concerns that are subject-specific and *reflecting* a consideration for the importance of their subject area perspectives and professional needs.

THE ISSUE OF TIME TO A SOCIAL STUDIES TEACHER

For social studies teachers working in the field of history, *time* becomes a factor on three levels. First, there is the large issue of developing student awareness of what happens in the present as a product, whether intentional or not, of what happened in the past. We are not isolated in our present existence. As social beings, we have a heritage, whether morally correct or incorrect, that originated in the past in the same way that we, as people, are products of our own past.

The interconnected nature of historic events and a time frame that includes a substantial knowledge of the "before" buttresses student understandings as they construct and give meaning to their personal interpretations. Many social studies teachers see the need to approach teaching by creating a *chronology* of the past coupled with a constant comparison with the world of the present. This assessment is not unique to those in social studies teaching history, but it is clearly a constant in courses dealing with cultural understanding and in the various social sciences such as sociology, psychology, politics, and economics.

On a second level, we see the relationship between time and the age of our students. As teachers, it is imperative that we find ways to assist our students as they construct a realization of the issue of time and how it bears significant importance in understanding their lives. This is one of the greatest strengths social studies has to offer; this learning connects them to what has taken place in the past and adds to how they view their futures. Unfortunately, many students are not connected with what is taking place in their world and what is shaping their lives.

The issue of time has a third component that is shared by all teachers, not just social studies teachers. This has to do with a curriculum that has a distinct beginning and end point and covers a specific body of knowledge. Course content can be dictated, as we have pointed out earlier, by teacher, school, district, or state recommendations. Many teachers and students are tied to beginning at a certain point and ending at a prescribed point *and* to meeting the needs of an assessment instrument in the process. Again, time plays a part in organizing teachers' and students' lives.

THE ISSUE OF TIME TO AN ENGLISH TEACHER

For an English teacher, the issue of time is different than for the social studies teacher. Whereas chronology is of the essence in social studies instruction, language arts instruction is primarily curricular; however, chronology can touch language arts in thematic ways. For example, in a unit on war, students may read Stephen Crane's *The Red Badge of Courage* (1964/1895), Erich Maria Remarque's *All Quiet on the Western Front* (1929), and Philip Caputo's *A Rumor of War* (1977). Although the emphasis in the study may be on the effects of war on humankind, the nature of human courage and bravery, the stress in life-threatening situations, or a myriad of other related themes, an important issue will be the time of the event. Questions to consider might be: "In what ways might the characters have been influenced by the times in which they live?" "Would the attitudes and emotions of Henry Fleming have been different if he were in Vietnam?" "Were the attitudes of the young soldiers in *All Quiet* different from those of the young marines in *Rumor?*"

Obvious linkages can be made to social studies in this area, even though the province of the social studies teacher is to examine the times that caused the wars and motivated the men to fight, whereas in the English class the emphasis is on the personal emotions and the choices the confrontation demanded. However, do not choices create actions, which in turn create history? At what point, then, do the boundaries become blurred on the thematic and conceptual level as students ponder the meaning and effect of war on society and on individuals?

English teachers are bound by time, as are social studies teachers, science teachers, mathematics teachers, and all others who follow a prescribed curriculum. Coverage, as explored earlier, makes time a real issue; but it is an issue that must be examined more closely in term of both the structure of the school day and the length of the school year. If teachers are creatures of their habitat, how do we change the habitat to address these issues? In Part II, we look more closely at alternatives available to school communities that are serious about making changes.

COMMON GROUND: THE IDEA OF BEING AGE-APPROPRIATE

The issue of time and place gives English teachers and social studies teachers an opportunity to connect in ways that will benefit their students immediately and nurture further linkages in the longer term. To go back to our earlier example of ninth-grade English and social studies teachers, we would find that they are dealing with students who are fourteen or fifteen years old. If we assume age is one of many indicators of intellectual maturity, we would not expect our students to handle tasks or view what they learn from the perspective of a forty-year-old much as we do not expect a forty-year-old to view the world as it would be viewed by a ninety-year-old. What is age-appropriate and intellectually accessible to students should concern all teachers. We would not expect a sixth-grade student to arrive at the same level of sophisticated conceptual understandings as a ninth grader should demonstrate.

Likewise, the conceptual frameworks that students construct through their learning in English or social studies may well surpass the expectations of the individual teacher. Success in English does not always indicate success in social studies. Differing motivations and personal student interests have a bearing on the results as well as on aptitude and effort. Consequently, in a team approach, students are offered a stronger sense of balance as they make links and see broader relationships. The dialogue about what expectations should be for students and how wide the possibilities are for student growth offer a starting point for building a sense of professional collaboration between English and social studies teachers that benefits both the individual student and the school.

FINDING A COMMON GROUND: DEVELOPING A SCOPE AND SEQUENCE OF FACTS, SKILLS, AND CONCEPTS

> *"I wish more of my classes would work together with other classes. We don't do that nearly enough but it makes things make more sense."*
>
> "Adam"

English teachers and social studies teachers, working in the same school and with the same student populations, yet addressing what they consider distinct subject matter, might do well to investigate what their peers are doing in their classrooms. Teachers who make such an inquiry of their fellow educators will find common skills and themes. Our backgrounds offer evidence that there is at least as much collective crossover in an English and social studies curriculum as there is uniqueness; what usually remains separate, however, is the factual material particular to the subject area. For example, direct information about a particular time or place in a history or geography class, including information such as the dates, figures, labels, or ordering of events, would be of primary interest to the social studies class. In the same vein, an English teacher may have items of specific interest, such as understanding of a part of speech, a writing style, or a particular genre of literature. Closer inspection of a curriculum may also indicate crossover in this area. For years, schools have attempted to emphasize writing across the curriculum, which ideally has all subject-area teachers emphasizing good writing skills. Additionally, in both English and social studies, a primary aim is to break down text to gain understanding and insight. More similarities can quickly be found in the skill and content areas represented in the two class outlines in areas such as researching, gathering and interpreting data, presenting data, and synthesizing on a higher level through student-created concepts. We remind the reader of our earlier discussion of beginning with skills and leading to conceptual understandings in setting up the building blocks for complementary and collaborative curriculum.

Learning Skills

The skills area offers a dual viewpoint of what takes place in a heterogeneous classroom. Again, imagine that we are looking at the work of ninth-grade English and social studies teachers. At a beginning level, both teachers encourage styles of behavior that foster the smooth operation of a cooperative classroom in which students share their learning in a spirit of collaboration. These behaviors stress responsibility to oneself and to the group. They represent skills necessary for success in the classroom and in life.

We would expect to find additional skills that are learning-specific being stressed in both classrooms. These areas might be based in topics such as conducting research, making presentations, writing for an audience, and writing to report. Other skill activities might include webbing, outlining, organizing information, approaching information, and problem solving, among others.

At this point, we encourage teachers to take their inquiry a step further and begin to build a *scope* and *sequence* of skills, making sure to note when each skill is introduced, when it is reinforced, and when mastery is expected. Likewise, the two teachers would also include their individual types of assessment for measuring student progress and skills mastery. Figure 1–1 and 1–2 offer a sample of skills drawn from the curriculum used by a high school English teacher and a social studies teacher working with students at the same grade level. We note not only the commonness of skills, but also the related *themes* that these skills follow in the work of each teacher. Such a situation is ripe for the beginning of teacher collaboration and team building.

Conceptual Understandings

If we continued to analyze the components of each class, we would begin to see patterns representing conceptual understandings. These patterns constitute understandings represented by ideas and relationships that are common to both subject areas as well as some that are subject-specific. For purposes of this book, we use our earlier working definition (Nowicki & Meehan, 1996, p. 15), which includes the following elements:

• concepts are ideas in a basic sense;

• the ideas that frame a concept include the interconnections of many

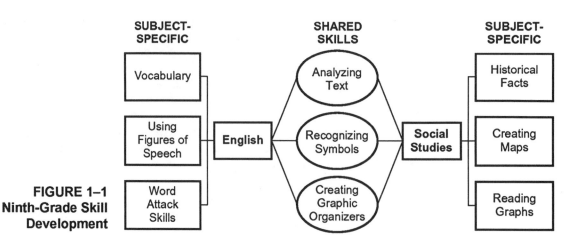

**FIGURE 1–1
Ninth-Grade Skill
Development**

diverse perspectives; We find this particularly true in the diversity
represented within a mixed-ability classroom;

- concepts are complex in that they require the support of other types
  of learning, such as other skills and factual information;

- concepts not only represent singular ideas in the social studies,
  but also complex interconnections which provide understandings
  accessible only by taking into account many separate ideas;

- concepts are continuous recreations in which students and teachers redefine and create the possibilities of learning;

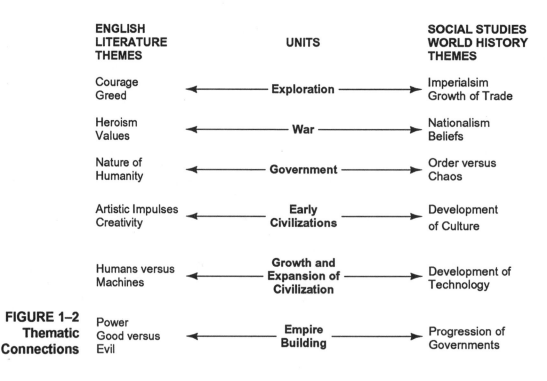

**FIGURE 1–2
Thematic
Connections**

- understanding a concept provides students with the *larger picture* of what they are doing in class as it is *tied* to their world. Concepts are grounded ultimately in the experience of living and the experience of learning.

The common ground conceptual understandings represent the crossover often encountered in higher level thinking. Some issues, such as the relationship between social order and chaos, are not subject-specific but are conceptual understandings common to both social studies and English. This issue is found in virtually every civilization in history and in the literature of many language arts classes, in works such as *Animal Farm* (1946), *Lord of the Flies* (1954), and *A Farewell to Arms* (1929). Furthermore, it represents a *unifying theme* between the two subject areas. Figure 1–3 presents ways that common conceptual understandings found in both curricula might be represented. As with learning skills, *common themes* are clearly evident. Combined with learning skills, conceptual understandings offer unlimited opportunities for collaborative work between two teachers.

Factual Content

Only now do we return to the issue of factual content. Although factual content may offer many crossover opportunities, for the most part it remains the province of each subject area. We have left this area of learning for the end of this discussion because for far too long this area alone has dominated what educators and society at large have considered learning to be. We do not agree. In our view, there needs to be balance and harmony between the three areas. Students need to know facts to have a working facility with the vocabulary of the unit, but the facts should be a starting point, not an ending or, as has often been the case, the only foundation for assessment of student learning. In Chapter 2, we offer a model for integrating factual knowledge into the blend of learning that takes place in a classroom. We offer methodology that can be used to promote unity between teachers rather than maintaining the impenetrable boundaries that too often exist. Now, having laid the foundations for bringing teachers together, we need to stop and assess our progress.

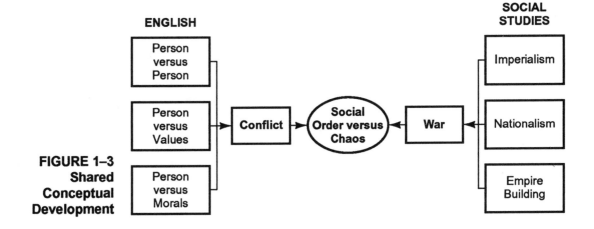

**FIGURE 1–3
Shared
Conceptual
Development**

TEAMING OR TEAM TEACHING?

We have both worked in *teaming* situations and in *team teaching* experiences. These are not the same; each offers its own unique benefits to teachers and students alike. In our experience, teaming involves teachers working together to meet students' needs. It gives teachers the opportunity to coordinate their respective work so it reaches students in an optimum manner and at an ideal time. While teaming requires a close, collaborative relationship between two teachers, it also allows them to maintain their individuality in defining their own classroom. Teaming is flexible enough to permit teachers to bring students together in shared classroom settings.

Team teaching means that two or more teachers directly share educational responsibility, including planning and curriculum. Teaming can lead to team teaching; in our view, however, team teaching is a more difficult achievement at the secondary level, although it is possible. For example, one author (Joe Nowicki) worked in a team-teaching experience that linked a senior-level English class with senior-level law class in a course called "Shakespeare and the Law," which was designed and taught by two teachers. This demanded significant accommodation from the schedule makers within the school.

Students benefit from both teaming and team teaching. Both arrangements are well suited for use in heterogeneous, nontracked schools. To build such relationships, teachers need the help of schedule designers and administrative leadership (e.g., Wheelock, 1992, p. 147). Teachers should begin with their curriculum and what they do in the classroom as they find commonality in their work. They should also develop a respect for their diversity as practitioners and for the perspectives each brings to such a collaborative relationship.

A Note about Administrative Assistance

*"We can't do it by ourselves. We need the
principal to get out of her office and help us!*
Mr. "A"

As stated previously, many schools are still governed by rigid bureaucratic structures that isolate students not only from each other but from teachers as well. Consequently, teachers become creatures of their habitat, of which too often they are not in control. They function in their own world and tend to follow whatever has worked in the past, over which they feel mastery. Busy with day-to-day activities, many teachers have neither the time or the energy to be educational researchers or to participate in discussions of the latest educational research or methodology.

Compounding this problem are those teachers who are becoming a so-called gray majority. Teaching for twenty-plus years, many feel they have paid their dues in professional developments and no longer want to take courses. As a result, many are only hazily aware of newer and perhaps better ways of doing things. However, despite these attitudes, the literature (e.g., Bolman & Deal, 1994) and experience suggest that teachers are willing to collaborate as team members or as team teachers. To do this successfully, they need cooperative administrators to help them in a number of ways. First, administrators must establish stimulating, thought-provoking workshops and inservices where teachers can learn about methodology from other practitioners and about theory from researchers. Administrators must support teachers with release time and a demonstrated willingness to restructure schedules and to replace traditional ways of doing things with newer models. They must be willing to risk success. Blase and Kirby (1992) remind us that "Effective principals consistently model appropriate behavior. They place themselves on exhibit as a portfolio of one" (p. 33). Administrators also need the support of superintendents and boards of education to be educational leaders and not mere managers or foremen in a traditional manufacturing hierarchy.

RECOGNIZING DIVERSITY IN THE CLASSROOM AND IN THE SCHOOL

Throughout this book, we focus on the strength of teachers working together in a participatory relationship. Collaborative work between teachers not only is suited to the heterogeneous classroom, but directly addresses the issues of diversity that confront schools today. These issues are particularly evident when considering the types of learning that take place in classrooms and how teachers working together can utilize course material to benefit all students.

The model we propose recognizes the broad diversity of student population in terms of gender, ethnicity and cultural heritage, learning styles and various intellectual skills, ways of viewing the world, and contributions that can be made to others. Schools are filled with exciting and unique populations that, given their experiences and perspectives, have an enormous amount to share with others. The shared responses to what is learned from such a mixed group constitute a valid and dynamic resource for our schools. The challenge is to develop mechanisms in school that access the diversity and encourage its input.

It is crucial to allow teachers to represent diversity in their teaching while modeling the behaviors of respect, tolerance, and cooperation that we hope to see manifested in our students. Teachers working to build models that include the academic, intellectual, and social needs of a multitude of learners will prepare classrooms for success in celebrating heterogeneity, rather than in limiting access based on homogeneity.

The Issue of Ability

> *"I think heterogeneous grouping is a lot better than homogeneous grouping. My other school was tracked. It means that more kids in that school gave up. And it was very cliquey. Almost everybody tries here.*
>
> "Tim"

The debate about nontracked classrooms that reflect heterogeneity is not over, nor will it be concluded soon. It is not the purpose of this book to present the arguments for and against tracking in schools. There is strong evidence, including the work of Jeannie Oakes (1985) and continuing through more recent work by Reba Neukom Page (1991) and Anne Wheelock (1992), that tracking is not a productive arrangement for organizing students and teachers. Our professional experience and reports from many others working in heterogeneous classrooms support contentions from the literature about the positive nature of nontracked schools.

The ability question has been a factor in developing our proposal. In particular, this book offers a collaborative model for teachers that can reach the upper level of success only in classrooms that are *not* homogeneous in terms of ability. Our model respects and celebrates the heterogeneity that can only come from classrooms representing a diverse group of learners. Our classroom work with our model tells us that these nontracked classrooms offer a realistic diversity in learning styles that is reflective of our society. Likewise, our model includes all learners as cooperative and collaborative participants in their learning. The lessons patterned on our model respect individual creativity rather than excluding some students on the basis of some arbitrary, artificial measure of ability. We offer lessons that allow for all students to be challenged to the limits of their ability while functioning together in a positive, harmonious environment. Furthermore, we offer lessons in which individual needs are met both through sharing and through individual effort, lessons that offer proof that cooperative teaching does not just mean using brighter students to teach slower ones. Additionally, these models allow for the fuller use of the various types of intelligence delineated by Howard Gardner (1989) and represented by Lazear (1991a, 1991b).

Concerns about Advanced Placement Students

Our position seems to beg the question "What about advanced placement (AP) students?" Our answer is that the models we present, including the lessons that compose them, reinforce our view that all students are "advanced placement" students, capable of higher level thinking and learning. This belief is grounded in our classroom experience and that of our peers in our own school and in others. We feel that all students can be challenged individually while being part of a collaborative group of learners, without hindering or slowing the pace of the acquisition of knowledge.

WHAT ABOUT ASSESSMENT?

The unit lessons we offer demonstrate the model we will present in the next chapter and include an assessment component. Assessment should not be excluded, nor should it be relegated to the end of the unit activities section. Assessment is based on the outcomes we expect. Teachers must know the expected outcomes as they design their units. They must be able to state precisely what specific facts, skills, and concepts they are developing in their lessons. Students also must know what is expected of them. Both students and teachers need to know the expected outcome before engaging in a task, rather than simply blundering down an obstacle-laden path with no map and no destination.

In any classroom, every activity needs to have an assessment component. The assessment must utilize students' and teachers' expertise, creativity, and effort as well as reflect and encourage the many creative realities that make up our classrooms.

Accountability

Our acknowledgment of the importance of assessment leads us to the issue of accountability. Students and teachers should be held accountable for their *investment, involvement,* and *gain* in their learning and in their teaching. This is especially true in nontracked classrooms. We do not see measuring what is learned as necessarily a function of a single test score, although we do utilize tests. Any measurement of student achievement needs to reflect many factors, including peer evaluation, self-evaluation, teacher evaluation, portfolios, demonstrations, and writing, as well as traditional assessments from teacher-prepared objective tests.

TOWARD THE COOPERATIVE SCHOOL

"I don't agree with labeling people at all. I think everybody should be mixed up in classes. Some people need extra help, but they can get that from their classmates. You know if you need help you go to anybody else in the class and they'll give it to you."

"Abby"

Schools should be places that reflect and model the best of what we as a society have to offer each other, rather than institutions in which diversity is used to divide us. We need to connect with each other as students and teachers and pool our strengths rather than letting those strengths be lost because of the outdated ideals of a bygone era. Cooperative and collaborative schools offer a powerful alternative for creating a future in which people will be able to achieve their individual potentials.

Faculties, Schools, Society, and Change: Teachers Modeling the Behavior Expected from Students

To move toward a society that reflects the strengths we share, we need schools that accentuate our strengths rather than our weaknesses. Working together is a tradition in other spheres such as industry and politics. Our model and our strategies seek to reinforce this approach for schools. Teachers need to be collaborative specialists rather than isolated experts. Modeling collaborative behavior will encourage their students to do the same.

In the next chapter, we present a model that encourages teachers and students to work together. It offers an explicit plan for utilizing student and teacher strengths to benefit all. Later chapters will highlight definitive theme-based strategies patterned on the model, which can be used in schools today.

CHAPTER 2

Creating a Model

*"Working together and sharing what we do
has brought us incredible energy and options
we never thought of before. It's exciting!"*

Ms. "K"

AN OVERVIEW

Throughout the first chapter of this book, we offered educators a rationale for setting up opportunities that foster interdisciplinary work between English and social studies teachers. Along with recognizing some areas in which differences are evident, we also noted many more places where similarities exist between teachers. As our suggestions indicate, we feel that empowering English and social studies teachers through the process of working together benefits students, teachers, and the entire school community. In this chapter, we will outline a set of steps to develop a model that connects rather than separates teachers. This model and its related framework provide the basis for the specific thematic strategies we now highlight.

One essential point is that in our model the issue of heterogeneity in classrooms is taken for granted; it is the underlying focus of this book. Our models, strategies, and frameworks are geared toward classrooms that are not tracked. We consider the issue of bringing heterogeneous grouping to homogeneous or tracked junior and senior high schools as an example of school change that fits well within the rubric of restructuring. Such changes actually restructure existing relationships within the organization and culture of a school community as well as within the academic philosophy (Nowicki, 1992, 1993; Nowicki & Felton, 1991). The models we offer deal directly with the issues raised by educators who have attempted to untrack only to ask, "What do we do now?"

We hope that this chapter and the second part of this book will provide some profitable insights and answer questions about developing lessons and methodology for creating a student- and activity-centered classroom in which all students are involved in their education.

THE UNIQUENESS OF EVERY SCHOOL COMMUNITY

Our combined professional experience has included teaching and administrating in more than a half dozen schools, and as workshop presenters, with educators representing more than two hundred schools. From these contacts, our conclusion is that no two schools are exactly alike. Each has a culture that reflects individuality and particular approaches to meeting the needs of its own educational community. Likewise, because we recognize that each school situation is unique, any model will need to be modified to answer the concerns of a particular community of students and teachers. Consequently, it is important to offer a framework supporting a set of models that teachers in many schools can use in creating collaborative work. The models we will present are meant to be flexible and practical so that teacher practitioners in individual schools can *put the models into practice*. We caution that any attempt to standardize an operational model without leaving room for classroom interpretation and restructuring suggests creating or continuing a tracked and rigid system.

Although we celebrate the diversity and uniqueness of schools, our experience also indicates similarities most schools share. One area of similarity is found in organizational strategies, such as tracks. Often we find common issues at many schools related to scheduling, to evaluation and assessment, and to the social well-being of the school community. Teachers from many different schools voice similar concerns about issues and events that affect their lives and those of their students. Within these similarities, inherent in the experience of teaching is the strength of teaching. As we stated earlier, the models we propose are created to allow for the diversity inherent in educators to shine through, while capitalizing on the similarities intrinsic to the junior, middle, or senior high school level.

BEGINNING A DIALOGUE

A teacher attempting to alter curriculum or try a new classroom strategy often works alone, without the input of peers. Even though teachers might ask colleagues for cursory advice or students for their input and critique, the teachers often remain alone, working in the isolation that schools breed. We have heard this frustration from many educators and have experienced it ourselves, but rigid school structures offer no alternatives. It is no surprise that educational researchers, theorists, and practitioners in the field all agree that networking teachers offers enormous advantages over isolating them (Barth, 1988; Little, 1990).

Teachers need to develop and share in a dialogue that reflects their professional work and worth. As an example, we think about an experienced and highly motivated teacher (Nowicki, 1992) who had spent thirty-five years teaching high school English. This teacher would have merely taken the accumulated knowledge and methodology of thirty-five years of skilled, highly competent work into retirement. Instead, however, during the last five years of this teacher's career, in a school going through a radical philosophical change, the teacher began working on a team and, for the first time in a long career, actually sharing knowledge with five other teachers. The important thing was the act of engaging in focused *professional dialogue* with other teachers *on a regular basis*. Allowing such activity to take place must be one of the organizational ideals of any junior or senior high school.

"Working together as a team celebrates the idea of teachers as experts and professionals sharing a similar culture."

Mr. "N"

Our suggestion is not simply to develop dialogue between teachers but to allow them to work together directly and frequently, including situations in which teachers *team* in developing a scope and sequence of learning skills and curriculum or teach cooperatively created material following a common *theme* in their own classrooms. Our proposal also allows teachers in both similar and different subject areas to come together and engage in *team-teaching* activities as necessary and beneficial to students. All such activity is dependent on the development of a dialogue—professional conversation, grounded in shared subject matter such as skills, themes, and concepts, conducted between teachers on a regular basis.

Our experiences and those of other educators indicate that teachers working together as members of an effective team place an extremely high value on that membership and that activity. Teachers speak about the emotional and professional support as well as the strength gained from working directly with others. Teachers who have seen their collaborative experiences disappear through the rigidity of inflexible schedules or of managing administrators speak in angry and often hurt voices about the effects of the loss of teacher collaboration on students' affective and academic success. Strength and sustenance come from working together.

How To Talk: Some Suggestions

On the surface, giving teachers directions about how to hold a discussion seems ludicrous, because who is better suited to facilitate discussion than a teacher. Teachers are masters of conversation and interaction, which are the bedrock of their professional existence. But look more closely at the idea. For the most part, teachers exercise their professional strength in conversations with students, not with one another. After years of the isolation provided by a tracking bureaucracy, professional conversation is the exception rather than the rule.

Such conversation, when it does take place, may be filled with hedging. It is common to try to protect what we have and to reinforce the appropriateness of what we do rather than opening ourselves up to a public sharing of our work and ideas. Consequently, teachers engaging in a professional dialogue are hesitant to display their own vulnerability. At times, they seem afraid of the possibility of attack by colleagues. Unfortunately, some of their fears are well founded, as others, protecting their own space, dismiss or disparage the ideas of their peers. Stung by previous criticisms and insensitivities, teachers may retreat deeper into their isolation.

To begin a dialogue, teachers need to develop a few ground rules, in much the same way as they would develop guidelines for students working in cooperative and collaborative groups. Each teacher needs to develop a respect for the unique perspectives held by others. At this point, teachers also need to focus on the similarities of what they do well and to respect and utilize the strength of differences manifested by the various discipline areas that are pivotal to creating the opportunity for interdisciplinary activity.

One way to develop similarities in what teachers do is by using a model in which teachers approach their subject matter through *theme*. The interrelatedness and common lines of dealing with skill-based and conceptual issues reflect clear, concise themes that a focused and regular dialogue conducted between teachers will identify. This dialogue must ultimately be designed to meet the needs of students as well as those of teachers as they work out *professionally cooperative* and *supportive* relationships. Open communication, beyond the realm of self-interest, can have powerful positive effects on teachers and their students.

Organizational and bureaucratic issues, such as scheduling, can short-circuit developing a framework and building a model. Teachers' concerns also include the amount and quality of support from the building-level administrator and the superintendent's office in allowing teachers to develop a sense of *shared time*. These problems must be addressed by each side in a spirit of mutual respect for the uniqueness of each other's responsibilities. These important issues must be clarified at each step in the creation of a model. Collaboration needs to be modeled between teachers and administrators as well as among teachers. Teachers who wish to design strategy-specific models must be willing to take the personal steps necessary to create an intraschool dialogue that is professionally collaborative and professionally supportive (Griffin, 1990; Evans, 1991).

STAGES OF DEVELOPING A MODEL FOR YOUR SCHOOL

Certain steps will facilitate the development of a collaborative thematic model between a language arts and social studies teacher. Although some of these may seem self-evident and based on common sense, a comprehensive listing establishes a clear direction for the participants. No one step is more important than the next; they serve as building blocks for each other, creating a harmonious flow and rhythm to the process. Some steps in the model have already been discussed; others we will introduce and detail. We expect an English and social studies teacher to address these steps in some way as they begin framing an interdisciplinary and thematic model for use in their classrooms.

The List

1. Develop a dialogue that offers teachers the chance to share their work without fear of criticism.

2. Set high expectations for students and for one another.

3. Provide time for this dialogue to occur daily, or at least on a regular, frequent basis.

4. Have each teacher contribute a scope and sequence of learning skills and of curriculum content from the current course of studies.

5. From the scope and sequence, note the commonalities. Identify themes and skills that are consistent to both disciplines and separate these

from subject-specific materials. Begin to fit skills and conceptual material around the similar themes.

6. Note the educational goals and student-centered outcomes in theme-based activity. Once student-centered outcomes have been established, develop a set of goals dealing with assessment that relate to the way learning activities would be designed within the theme.

7. Construct a thematic scope and sequence, including what material is to be taught by each teacher and when. This should include forms of assessment, a brief outline of skill development activities, concepts, and subject-specific facts.

8. Outline a plan that focuses on the issue of time. Such a plan would detail the amount of separate teaching time and common teaching time.

9. Create subject-specific teaching strategies that can be applied in a collaborative and heterogeneous classroom to meet the needs of all learners. Note that some methodology is adaptable to both areas.

10. Involve administrators and schedulers in developing your plan. Do not let scheduling issues destroy your plans. Look for subtle openings that can allow for student and teacher interaction with a common theme at some level.

11. Involve and inform students and parents (see Figure 2–1).

We have found these steps a valuable progression in developing thematic units with students at the same grade levels. Much of what we suggest has been born of trial and error. We speak from our own levels of frustration at the way events have turned out as a result of the limiting aspects of school organization. However, these steps should be both a springboard and a guidepost for building interdisciplinary themes.

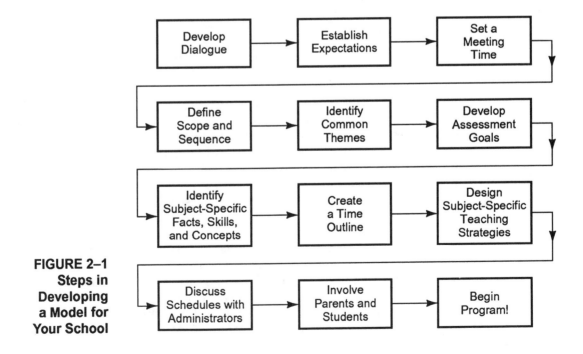

**FIGURE 2–1
Steps in
Developing
a Model for
Your School**

THE SCOPE AND SEQUENCE

The center and the core of an English–social studies thematic unit is the scope and sequence, which should serve as the blueprint each class and teacher will follow together. The scope and sequence lets teachers know where they are relative to material coverage, details when new information will be introduced, and reinforces earlier learning. It provides a clear statement about the subject-specific facts and also highlights the *shared* conceptual understandings buttressing the theme. In addition, the respect each teacher holds for the perspectives of the other must be evident. Because the scope and sequence is for the two involved teachers, it must be in a form that is easily read. We offer two sample formats to stimulate thinking in these terms. Figure 2–2 is a more complete, long-term unit document; Figure 2–3 is an abbreviated short-term unit possibility.

GRADING AND ASSESSMENT IN THE SCOPE AND SEQUENCE

A second key component for developing a thematic unit focuses on the issue of grading. In many ways, grading based on an idea of evaluation as a mechanism for sorting and separating students represents a connection to models that are not compatible with nontracked schools. This is not to say that schools or teachers should not engage in some form of assessment. They should. Assessment is one of the necessary duties of teachers. It must be informative and evaluative, however, not merely a way of ranking students.

> *"Heterogeneous grouping has made me realize that there is more than one way to evaluate kids. It isn't just test! test! test!"*
>
> Ms. "R"

Assessment practices in the heterogeneous classroom should focus on helping students improve and sharpen their skills and understanding. How students are assessed needs to be linked directly to the goals of the thematic unit. These goals need to be student-centered and focused on reflecting the success, effort, and achievement of individual students. Assessment practices should be tied not only to the goals generated for students through the activity, but also to the *outcomes* that are produced by meeting the goals.

The reliance on goals and outcomes is crucial to developing assessment tools and activities in the heterogeneous classroom. To focus on interdisciplinary and thematic units, outcomes must be stated and planned from the beginning of the unit. Assessment for mastery becomes a process that is integral to the multidimensional thematic unit. It becomes a recognized part of students' learning rather than a single evaluation component at the end of a monodimensional, single-perspective unit.

FIGURE 2–2

SOCIAL STUDIES SUBJECT-SPECFIC	Time	Activities	Common Links	Activities	Time	ENGLISH SUBJECT-SPECFIC
Facts → People, places, events, decisions, alliances, statistics, casualties. Date, treaties	WK 1	• Students working cooperatively will define terms of unit.	*Focus Points:* • Social, political, and economic conditions in Europe in late 1800s.	Students will read four short stories with themes of survival, conflict, societal change, and individual struggle.	Weeks 1–3	**→ Facts** Literary terms Such as character, setting, tone, point of view, climax
	WK 1	• Students will create a timeline from 1880s to 1940s.	• Causes of World War I	Students will read a novel outside of class with a theme of war **and** create final activity on novel.	Weeks 1–4	Vocabulary of Readings, Authors
Skills Creating timelines Cartography Reading charts Creating historical personae	WK 2	• Students will draw maps of pre- and postwar Europe.	• Impact of war on society • Effects of World War I on the world			**↓ Skills** Critical reading Cooperative work Manipulating facts and concepts through organizers
	WK 3	• Students will present 4- to 6-minute "Who am I?"	**Interdisciplinary Objectives:** • Students will develop an understanding of connections between English and Social Studies.	Students will read poetry and songs of war and create their own.	1 Week	**→ Concepts** Literature as means of seeking truth Conflict Role of individual within society
Concepts Role of historical change Nationalism War/conflict Injustice	WK 4	• Students will re-create and role-play Paris Peace Talks.	• Students will work with cause-and-effect relationships. • Students will develop frameworks for presenting material.	Students will create a period piece of writing on war.	1 Week	
				Students will create a documentary of Paris Peace Talks.	Week 4	

Common Themes

— Humans' inhumanity to fellow humans
— Conflict of good versus evil
— How war dehumanizes people
— Need, will to survive
— Heroism and courage

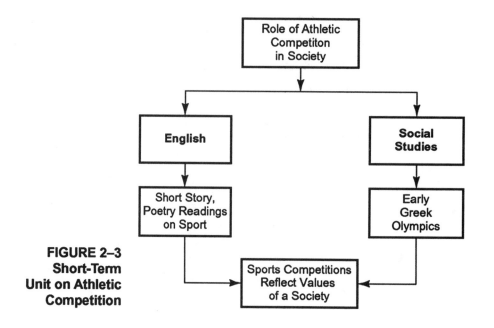

**FIGURE 2–3
Short-Term
Unit on Athletic
Competition**

In order for assessment strategies to be a key part of the process of thematic and interdisciplinary learning, they need to be linked to the teaching–learning activities employed in the classroom. In this way, they are a continuous element emphasizing a progression based on acquisition of facts and skills that lead to the higher level of synthesis and production of knowledge. In this way, also, assessment is part of progressive mastery of skills, facts, and concepts, not an end in itself.

If assessment is to benefit all students, it needs to focus on individuals rather than on a comparison of students. This does not mean doing away with student accountability. On the contrary, basing assessment on individual students increases accountability while giving students immediate feedback and an individualized constructive critique. The lessons that make up sections in our sample unit all carry components that identify their elements and offer a guide for assessment. They are based on mastering factual information, skills, and conceptual understandings that are identified in the scope and sequence and represent outcomes for the unit collaboratively established at the beginning of instruction.

COMPROMISE FROM THE MASTER SCHEDULER

*"You know, we lost our team because it didn't
fit into the schedule for the rest of the school."*
Mr. "L"

The person who develops the schedule for a school exerts a great deal of control over the school. The scheduler assigns teachers to classrooms and can determine what teachers can teach, both within and outside their discipline. A schedule determines when teachers meet, if there is common planning time, and when someone eats lunch. The list could go on and on, but it is enough to say that the person making the schedule does have considerable power.

Scheduling is often a thankless job. No one person can always please everyone. The response to scheduling by a teaching staff is often less than enthusiastic. In such situations, it is understandable that the scheduler, whether an administrator or a guidance counselor, becomes defensive and unreachable. These responses are often interpreted by those affected by the schedule as unsympathetic to the overall needs of the building. The message is often clear: The building must function, and students and teachers are of secondary importance in the old-fashioned manufacturing organizational model we described in Chapter 1.

The traditional tracked school prides itself on efficiency and organization in scheduling. Such a schedule sets a tone for the organization that does not reflect the needs of a cooperative and collaborative school. To bring teachers together and open up opportunities for community growth within the school, room for compromise must exist in the schedule. Ideally, teacher assignment would provide for accommodations to allow teachers to work together on teams and would provide the common planning time necessary for professional interaction to occur. Not all schools, particularly at the high school level, have made these adjustments in the structure of the school day.

Other arrangements can be worked out within the schedule also, such as linking teachers of similar students in piggy-backed classes, having teachers who are working together on themes share the same room regardless of discipline, or arranging student schedules by classes working on thematic issues rather than by a singleton course. Still other alterations in a schedule can include the time and length of classes, their rotation, and their position in the day. To say that the schedule cannot be modified is more an admission of inadequacy than an assessment of the feasibility of two teachers building a thematic unit.

It should be obvious by now that the one issue that often dominates scheduling, that of arranging a school according to tracks, is not part of our discussion of obstacles to developing interdisciplinary themes. It doesn't factor in. Ideally, all students would be working through interdisciplinary themes, which would make scheduling even easier.

We recognize that we do not live in an ideal world and that educational scheduling is far from an exact science. It would be inappropriate for us to advocate for schedule change without offering suggestions of our own. Schedules 2–1, 2–2, and 2–3 represent overviews that offer advice rather than explicit solutions. They may be appropriate for some schools and not for others, not a surprising observation given our belief in the uniqueness of all schools in the situations they face. Flexible schedules represent an opening of the door, leading to compromises that can benefit students.

SCHEDULE 2–1   Schedule Possibilities: Scenario #1

Given a standard schedule based on seven periods a day:

Block 1   8:00–8:45
Block 2   8:50–9:35
Block 3   9:40–10:25
Block 4   10:30–11:15
Block 5   11:20–12:45
Block 6   12.50–1:35
Block 7   1:40–2:25

Our suggestion is that for four days or a full week each month, two blocks be dedicated to interdisciplinary activity linking at least two classes throughout the school. Following a standard Monday schedule, teachers would negotiate for interdisciplinary space. Administrators would ensure that all teachers participated during the year and that all teachers had an opportunity to mesh their work with another's. For example, social studies teachers may claim Blocks 1 and 2 for the first month. Other arrangements based on proposals from the teacher would follow. For the rest of the day, after Blocks 1 and 2, the rest of the school could return to the standard school day.

	M	T	W	Th	F
8:00–8:45					
8:50–9:35					
9:40–10:25	A	B	C	D	E
10:30–11:15	B	C	D	E	A
11:20–12:45	C	D	E	A	B
12:50–1:35	D	E	A	B	C
1:40–2:25	E	A	B	C	D

Lunch Rotation (label at left of table, rows 11:20–12:45 area)

SCHEDULE 2–2   **Schedule Possibilities: Scenario #2**

Given a standard schedule based on seven periods a day:

Block 1   8:00–8:45
Block 2   8:50–9:35
Block 3   9:40–10:25
Block 4   10:30–11:15
Block 5   11:20–12:45
Block 6   12.50–1:35
Block 7   1:40–2:25

In this scenario, students in Grade 9 all have social studies and English during Blocks 1, 2, and 3. Students in Grade 10 have social studies and English during Blocks 5, 6, and 7. Students in Grade 11 have classes in Blocks 1, 2, and 3. Seniors have their classes dealing with the two disciplines during Blocks 5, 6, and 7. Blocks utilizing the three periods will be constructed during the school year and offer various possibilities for interdisciplinary activity.

		M	T	W	Th	F
1	8:00–8:45	Grade	Grade	Grade	Grade	Grade
2	8:50–9:35	9 / Grade	9 / Grade	9 / Grade	9 / Grade	9 / Grade
3	9:40–10:25	11	11	11	11	11
4	10:30–11:15	LUNCH ROTATION →				
5	11:20–12:45	Grade	Grade	Grade	Grade	Grade
6	12:50–1:35	10 / Grade	10 / Grade	10 / Grade	10 / Grade	10 / Grade
7	1:40–2:25	12	12	12	12	12

SCHEDULE 2–3   **Schedule Possibilities: Scenario #3**

Given a standard schedule based on seven periods a day:

Block 1   8:00–8:45
Block 2   8:50–9:35
Block 3   9:40–10:25
Block 4   10:30–11:15
Block 5   11:20–12:45
Block 6   12.50–1:35
Block 7   1:40–2:25

One week each month is dedicated to interdisciplinary activity. Teachers request time, and all students are assigned to a specific place and time.

THE ISSUE OF SHARED TIME

English teachers and social studies teachers working together on a common theme have the added responsibility of budgeting time for work dedicated to their particular subject area as well as to the common links that represent the thematic work. Working together might solve some of the problems associated with isolation, but it does not relieve a teacher of the burden of work. In fact, it creates more work. Yet to some outside the school community, efforts toward teaming are not seen as a wise use of available resources.

In one of our local junior high schools teachers work on grade-level teams. These teams, which have been in operation for more than five years, have been impressive. Teachers and students feel a bond with their team members. Strategies are developed that provide the expertise and perspectives of various team members to identify and assist students with their learning. Yet despite a mountain of evidence supporting the use of teams, at budget time the team concept is the first to be placed on the budget cutters' chopping block. The rationale? Teaming is not cost-effective, as it means that teachers must have a common planning period during which they are not in the classroom with students. Such logic reinforces the efficiency model of a bureaucratic manufacturing structure.

The issue of efficiency or cost-effectiveness created by matching the maximum number of students with a set number of teachers is not geared to a heterogeneous model of arranging schools, although it is geared in many ways to tracked models. The issues in a heterogeneous school are not centered on control, whereby one teacher occupies the attention of many students for a certain amount of time. The focus, instead, is one in which the school, ideally, becomes a collaborative community of learners, and control is not a paramount issue. That is not to say that discipline is not problematic, as it is in any diverse community. How we deal with each other will always be a question in a democratic society. A perfect way to resolve the issue of respecting the rights of others while maintaining our own has not yet been developed, but models of organizing classrooms that rely on behavior control of a group by one person do not fit with the implications of the heterogeneous model.

Concerns over how teachers will use their time together in a collaborative effort should not be an issue. Instead of criticizing school districts that allow teachers to work together and, in fact, makes special provisions to encourage this practice, we should be celebrating their actions as innovative and forward-thinking. Teachers who already have the privilege of communication and collaboration, as well as those who wish to create situations that foster thematic interdisciplinary collaboration, need to make their case to parents, students, and others in the larger community. All too often, the issue of teacher time will focus the debate, especially for social studies and English teachers seeking collaboration.

SUPPORT FROM ADMINISTRATORS AND THE FRONT OFFICE

"We need someone to step in and be a strong person to solve the problem."

Ms. "P"

Any effort to alter the way relationships in a school are organized, such as implementing heterogeneous grouping practices, needs the support of the school administration. Principals and assistant principals must be supporters if teachers are to build interdisciplinary units based on common themes. Teachers need support in developing common planning time, developing curriculum, and resolving scheduling issues, among other areas.

Administrators connect the various things that take place in a school. They are the ones who provide a sense of physical and professional security (Blase & Kirby, 1992). Administrators do not need to be innovators in curriculum or in developing subject- or theme-specific teaching strategies; but they do need to be innovators in adapting the structure of the organization to the way members of the school community meet the demands of a society that becomes more and more needy every day. Administrators can link all teachers and students to a common focus. Their support for a form of innovation, such as creating thematic units, is essential for student and teacher success. Furthermore, administrators must be at a higher level as the curriculum coordinators within their schools. They have to address the deeper philosophical differences that might exist between English and social studies teachers. At a certain point, administrators may need to be the arbitrators between diverse points of view and establish the groundwork of a shared vision. Teachers should expect this type of support from those charged with monitoring the larger picture of the school community. Without their support, change is difficult, perhaps impossible.

What takes place in the front office also affects the English and social studies teachers working to build interdisciplinary themes into their curriculum for the benefit of creating collaborative schools. Districtwide administrators can offer support that brings substantial symbolic and practical worth. Those teachers who enjoy the support of district administrators will have an easier time enacting interdisciplinary and thematic units in their classrooms.

ADJUSTMENTS TO PERSONALIZE A PROGRAM

We began this chapter with a discussion of the uniqueness of individual schools and teachers. Such uniqueness represents a strength in our educational system, creating innovation, interpretation, and creativity among teachers and students. The model highlighted in this chapter is meant to serve as a fundamental guide for developing a thematic and interdisciplinary unit geared to the heterogeneous classroom, not a prescription. A thematic unit, particularly one that crosses disciplinary lines, should reflect the creativity that teachers develop and share as they take their disciplinary perspectives to the "marketplace" of interdisciplinary awareness. We envision English and social studies teachers using the models we will present as well as the frameworks that were highlighted in this chapter as a set of guideposts while they create an interdisciplinary curriculum that addresses the needs of their students. Teachers will always need to personalize their work if schools are to remain creative and vibrant places where learning is encouraged.

RESOURCES

Although we offer some specific titles that we believe work well or that are not widely anthologized as part of a traditional canon, we intentionally do not include a comprehensive or prescriptive bibliography for each unit. To do so might inhibit precisely the type of collegial activity we hope to encourage within schools. Many of the sources we and other teachers have used in creating lessons like those we describe are drawn from the brainstorming sessions that occur when English teachers, social studies teachers, and librarians come together for a common cause. Clearly, these educators are, in themselves, a veritable "book of lists," holding a wealth of information in their fields. Some of the best suggestions we have received about materials have come from the students. Additionally, the final selection of materials should be completed by those who best know the interests and abilities of their students.

A Note about Materials for Mixed-Ability Classrooms

Similarly, we hesitate to offer suggestions for differing levels. Again, teachers should consult with reading teachers, special-education personnel, and the librarian for a discussion of materials at varying levels to personalize programs for students at a variety of skill levels in their classes. In many ways, this is an opportunity for teachers and specialists, working together, to develop a collegial bibliography. Resource materials should address the topic of interdisciplinary study but should also reflect the diversity of learning styles in mixed-ability classrooms. For example, in an English situation, whereas some readers may have difficulty with *A Proud Taste for Scarlet and Miniver* in a medieval unit, *The Door in the Wall* is an easier but still excellent novel dealing with the same subject matter.

In social studies, a text may be a standard tool for the class, but the Eyewitness series, the Scholastic Book Services' set of books on Western European development, and Allyn and Bacon's Human Adventure Series all offer substantial supporting material for different reading levels. As teachers continue to add materials—films such as *Ladyhawke;* videocassettes such as the A&E "Biography" series, which is available for purchase; music, drama, and art; and books on tape, captioned tapes, and abridged versions or retellings—the possibilities for engaging all levels are overwhelming. The underlying precept for establishing these materials is for teachers and specialists to talk and plan together for all students.

OUTCOMES AND EXPECTATIONS

"You know I don't read well but here I got to take a class with two teachers on Shakespeare and the law. I think I would have been in a slow group somewhere else and not been able to do that."

"Petey"

The next part of this book demonstrates the model we have suggested. We present six long-term units, forty short-term strategies, and twenty year-long themes applicable to thematic and interdisciplinary activity between English and social studies teachers in heterogeneous classrooms and nontracked schools. Our focus includes the recognition that comes with developing shared expectations and then envisioning measurable outcomes that reinforce the need to respect the nature of student-centered activities. The activities we build into our models celebrate the diversity brought to classrooms by students and by teachers. In fact, recognition of the diversity of learning styles brought by all students to their classrooms occupies a central point in the strategies we suggest and in the outcomes we propose. There is a clear connection between the expectations we set as educators and the successes of our students engaged in classroom activity. This level of expectation is especially true in a mixed-ability classroom, where teachers must set high standards for all students, respecting individual differences. We have found, repeatedly, that students will perform up to the level of expectation, if those expectations are personalized, understood, and accepted as a part of the assessment process.

CHAPTER 3

Short-Term Themes

INTRODUCTION

> *"I like working with other kids, that's why I like this place. It [cooperative learning] makes it a lot easier to understand, and by teachers having us work together, it makes it easier to teach and to learn."*
>
> "Tiffany"

This chapter presents twenty strategies for interdisciplinary activity in cooperative and collaborative classrooms. The strategies and activities are organized around specific themes that apply to English and social studies classes. The activities, which range in length from one day to five weeks, are meant as a beginning point for teachers interested in developing an interdisciplinary dialogue.

We offer these strategies as guides and as a stimulus to conversations about methodology between teachers. Although we highlight only twenty, there are literally hundreds of interconnections that can be made between junior and senior high school English and social studies curricula. Ideally, we envision teachers doing what we expect students to do—to construct the content and relationships in their teaching as we expect students to construct meanings through their learning.

Some of the strategies are very specific; they offer daily activities, recommend amounts of time to spend, suggest materials, and include assessment criteria. Others are more general, offering a structure and a timeline but leaving materials and assessment up to the individual teachers and teams. This is intentional, as some teachers feel more confident in trying an activity that is highly directed, whereas others prefer only an outline. We offer something for each.

Our approach also is activity-centered. We strongly believe that students must be involved in their education. They must discover meaning, manipulate facts and statistics, apply their knowledge, and develop constructs that truly synthesize learning. As teachers, we must stimulate learning through the creation of activities that foster growth. We should not be like Procrustes, making our victims fit into our beds of knowledge.

We suggest that teachers try some of these strategies in their classrooms. Although some teachers may want to follow the strategies closely, others may wish to make modifications, and still others may wish to use our work merely as a group of suggestions that offer practical direction gained from experience. We are comfortable with whatever helps others to open new avenues in the teaching–learning process.

Title:	Medieval Verses
Subject Areas:	World History and English
Ages/Grades:	Grade 9
Number of Students:	40 (or two classes)
Focus Points:	1. Relating the time and place in history with styles of spoken reports
	2. Using verse as a source of information
	3. Noticing the changes in language over time
Time Necessary:	2 days

OVERVIEW

Using the theme of communicating through verse, this interdisciplinary activity allows two teachers to bring their classes together for a short time. In this exercise, students who share a world history class with one teacher and an English class with another teacher work for two days, four class periods, on a common topic. The students in social studies are studying the Middle Ages. In English they are working on a unit focusing on poetry.

On the first day and during the first class period, the students are given examples of verse often read during the Middle Ages, including material that was used to entertain as well as to inform. Students note both the structure of the verse and its content.

Students are then broken into groups of three and begin work on their own verse telling about an event that took place in medieval Europe. Teachers give each group of students four events to use as topics, as well as materials to conduct research on each of the topics assigned. The final products must each contain a minimum of five historical facts. With teacher assistance, each group develops three sets of verse with approximately 25 lines each. These should be completed by the end of the third class period.

The fourth class period, on the second day, is used by students to present their work to the rest of the class. Students turn in all three examples of verse they have completed but select one to present orally to the class. Each group splits their verse into three sections, with each member of the group reading one-third. Students then receive a checklist evaluation sheet to rate their own efforts and those of their groups.

INTERDISCIPLINARY OBJECTIVES

1. Students will understand the role of poetry in past society.

2. Students will translate the history of events through the spoken word and the written word.

3. Students will use verse to communicate a coherent thought.

4. Students will understand the logic of creating a verse.

COMMON LINKAGES

Materials

1. Examples of verse from the Middle Ages

2. Teacher-provided lists of historical events

Activities and Time

1. On the first day, students are introduced to examples of medieval verse and are divided into groups of three. This lasts one class period.

2. During the second class period on the first day, students receive a list of four potential topics from which they will select three. Students then begin their research to discover five facts about the event. Groups also begin to write the verse.

3. Students continue working in groups during the third class period, on the second day of the activity. Each group uses this time to complete its research and verse writing.

4. Students turn in all three verse selections but select only one to read to the class. Each student reads sections of the verse to the rest of the class. Before the end of the class, students are given an assessment checklist addressing the levels of group participation and individual contributions to the process. Each teacher also has the option of assigning additional activities, such as a reaction paper.

Factual Material

Elements associated with poetry and verse; more than 30 historical facts about the Middle Ages.

Skills

1. Writing verse

2. Incorporating facts into short spoken reports

3. Researching

4. Editing

5. Using collaborative work strategies

6. Presenting an oral report

Concepts

1. The connection between the written and the spoken word

2. The relationship between history and English verse

3. The developmental nature of communication

4. The impact of electronic technology on communication

Assessment

1. Teacher assessment of student-written verse with written reaction

2. Teacher assessment of student-spoken verse through written reaction

3. Teacher assessment of student group work through checklist

4. Student assessment of group work with checklist

5. Student self-assessment with checklist or narrative

Notes

This activity provides an opportunity for an English teacher and a social studies teacher to initiate an interdisciplinary dialogue around the theme of communicating through verse. Though brief, it engages students in a concentrated period of activity. The exercise provides an additional chance to focus on developing group and interpersonal skills.

This can truly be a *team teaching* experience in which two subject areas are focused on a common theme. The teachers need to find a common time in which they can bring students together to work. Although ideally the teachers would share the same students in separate classes, if this is impossible, a compromise might be needed in which groups representing a partial mix of students could be created. Also, creation of a grade-level team would facilitate activities like this one.

SHORT-TERM THEMES

Title:	Creation Stories
Subject Areas:	American Studies and English II (Creative Writing)
Ages/Grades:	Grade 11
Number of Students:	20
Focus Points:	1. The frequency of creation stories in many cultures
	2. Creation stories as a work of cultural history
	3. The art of writing creation stories
	4. Stories about the beginning of a people as a source of uniqueness regarding cultural heritage
	5. Recognition of ethnic and cultural diversity
Time Necessary:	3 days

OVERVIEW

This activity, lasting three days, brings together an American Studies class focusing on Native American history with an English class engaged in creative writing. Students will read the legends and tales of a number of ethnic groups that describe their cultural origins. Students then will write their own creation story based on criteria that they design. The stories might tell of their own origins, should be no more than five pages long and can be presented to the class on the third and final day of the activity.

Stories about the origin of a people often convey powerful images. These stories are filled with visual and descriptive scenes that come alive in either written or spoken words. They have their own logic and often express a lesson that those coming later are expected to follow and use as a basis for religion. In a sense, these stories are outlines that hold a society together through the generations.

Creation stories have a universal appeal. They are found on all continents. From North America, for example, creation stories abound in Native American tribal cultures, varying from tribe to tribe as an expression of the uniqueness of the tribes. From other continents and peoples come stories as diverse as those that buttress the Judeo-Christian tradition of Western civilization and those that organize the great peoples of Asia and Africa.

Because creation stories are widespread and figure prominently in world cultures, their study is applicable to a wide array of social studies and English classrooms. This activity focuses on one group of creation stories and on the images presented by Native American cultures. These stories offer an exceptional window to help students understand the way many of these peoples viewed the world and their place in it.

Assigning students the task of writing stories describing their own origins further helps them understand the meanings carried by creation stories. The acts of writing and reflection are essential in developing a story that vividly describes a beginning and provides moral lessons that serve as an outline for a later society.

Through the creative process, students take elements such as plot, setting, and characterization and put them directly into their own work. Although they are asked to tell a story, they are not simply telling a story but are crafting a work that celebrates their creativity.

INTERDISCIPLINARY OBJECTIVES

1. Students will develop a global view in terms of understanding the heritage of other cultures.

2. Students will develop creative writing skills.

3. Students will recognize the importance of diversity.

4. Students will present a personal statement to an audience.

COMMON LINKAGES

Materials

Various creation stories (provided by the teachers)

Activities and Time

1. On the first day of the activity, students are organized into groups of three. Each group is given six creation stories of moderate length. After an initial presentation by the teachers concerning the process of analysis involved in reading the stories effectively, the separate groups begin the reading and analysis. Students respond in a reader response journal.

2. The second day finds the students writing their own creation story based on the facts of their lives and family. They can expand it to include the larger society if their teachers wish. Rough drafts are submitted to group members for critical analysis. Teachers conference individually and support peer editing.

3. Students are expected to complete their stories by class time on the third day of the activity. They are then required either to read their stories to the class or to share their written work with their fellow group members and the larger class. Students expect to receive at least three written reactions by the end of class time. The teachers then collect the finished stories and offer their own reflections.

Factual Material

Information specific to the particular creation stories assigned, elements essential to developing creative writing skills.

Skills

1. Creative writing skills

2. Collaborative group work, including editing and analysis

3. Critical reading skills

Concepts

1. The universality of creation stories

2. The impact of legend on social structures

3. Diversity and similarity among various world cultures

4. The meanings within legends

Assessment

1. Written student reactions to the work of others

2. Written teacher assessment of students' writing

3. Teacher assessment of individual and group participation in the reading–writing process

Notes

Creation stories can be used at many different grade levels. We hope that the level of expectations set by the teachers matches the students' age and grade level as well as their individual levels. In this case, assume students will submit final products appropriate for eleventh-graders.

Our suggestion allows teachers to come together for a short period of time in a *team teaching* situation. This activity requires that teachers find a common time in which to share students. It may mean adjusting some schedules or altering what students normally do in a school day to create a common block of time.

The theme of this activity links English and social studies. It allows students to experience an important aspect of culture and to create their own understandings about themselves from what they have read.

Teachers should use their own background and those of their students in selecting a cross-section of creation stories. We recommend *Myths and Motifs in Literature,* edited by David Burrows, Frederick Lapides, and John T. Shawcross. We have had good success with "Origins of the World: Mission Indians of California," selections from Ovid's *Metamorphoses,* and "Genesis I and II," all of which are contained in *Myths and Motifs in Literature.*

SHORT-TERM THEMES

Title: William Shakespeare: Poet and Playwright

Subject Areas: World History and English 9

Ages/Grades: Grade 9

Number of Students: 20

Focus Points: 1. The life of William Shakespeare

2. Life in Elizabethan England

3. Literature during the Renaissance

Time Necessary: 3 weeks

OVERVIEW

This activity brings together students in ninth-grade World History and English classes in a study of William Shakespeare. It should come at a time in the school year when ninth-graders are about to read one of Shakespeare's works in an English class and are studying the Renaissance or Elizabethan England in a World History class. It can serve as a strong and focused introductory activity, which will give students a deeper understanding of Shakespeare's life and of the times in which he lived. This week-long study culminates in a student-produced documentary (see Nowicki & Meehan, 1996, for an elaboration of this type of strategy) that highlights students' efforts.

The activity involves students both as individuals and in groups. They will be responsible for discovering information that will then be translated into a presentation reflecting creativity and content.

In the case of a week-long documentary project, ninth graders are required to create a twenty-minute documentary about William Shakespeare, based on a certain number of videotaped segments. Students take part in the production as site reporters, in the roles of characters from Shakespeare's time being interviewed, as videographers, and as copywriters. All students are involved in research and editing. Students are organized in groups of five to seven who will be responsible for producing and filming the various segments of the video-documentary. The final product is viewed by all students at the end of the week.

INTERDISCIPLINARY OBJECTIVES

1. Students will gain historical background for reading the work of William Shakespeare.

2. Students will create a collaborative product.

3. Students will learn to present information in a video format.

4. Students will work with the genre of nonfiction.

COMMON LINKAGES

Materials

1. Various works dealing with the life of William Shakespeare

2. Reference materials, such as encyclopedias

3. Video camera, tape, monitor

4. Costumes (optional)

Activities and Time

1. Each day constitutes two class periods, one in English and one in social studies. On the first day, the teachers explain the activity to students; they make sure to tell students what the goals and expectations are. Students, divided into groups of five, are then assigned to build a timeline with twenty entries about the life of Shakespeare. The timelines are then displayed to the other groups in the class, and a larger, more inclusive class timeline is recorded. From the events on this timeline, six or seven major issues in the life of Shakespeare are selected. These constitute the areas of presentation in the documentary. Each student then selects one topic area to study. Some groups may need adjustment for size.

2. The second and third days of the activity find students researching their particular topics. Roles within the group are also divided so that these are interviewers, characters, videographers, and assistants.

3. On the fourth day, students edit their final copy. Depending on the number of participants, video segments may range from four to seven minutes long. Students rehearse their work and complete final preparations for costuming.

4. On the fifth day of the activity, groups rehearse their copy one more time and then begin filming the segments. Because film editing will be at a minimum, students may have only what they produce from a nonedited take. The class then watches the final product. Students are given a sheet with questions about William Shakespeare and an activity group assessment. Both are to be completed in class by the student.

Factual Material

William Shakespeare, Queen Elizabeth, 1564, The Globe, The Hope, The Swan, Anne Hathaway, James I, The King's Men, blank verse, Ben Johnson, Renaissance, London, Stratford on Avon, 1616, tragedy, comedy, sonnets, a selection of Shakespearean plays

Skills

1. Researching

2. Writing and editing

3. Working collaboratively

4. Videography

5. Critically reviewing

Concepts

1. The relationship of history to literature

2. A documentary

3. The Renaissance and literature

4. The relationship of politics to literature

Assessment

1. Student completion of teacher question sheet

2. Student assessment of group work

3. Student self-assessment

4. Teacher assessment of student presentation

5. Teacher assessment of individual contributions to group work.

Notes

This activity, based on an easily developed theme, provides an excellent introduction to a study of Shakespeare (or another author). It also serves to reinforce a study of the Renaissance and the Elizabethan period. Students are expected to generate enough information to produce a competent documentary. The information provided in the final documentary is an example of students serving as peer teachers. They are constructing their knowledge and helping others to do the same.

Students need clear expectations and goals at the beginning of the activity. They need to know what is expected for an outcome by the teachers. Attendance is crucial throughout the activity, and this needs to be stressed from the first day.

If teachers do not share the same group of students, they need to find a way of linking two classes in a common time. In these situations, as in others, a *team* of teachers arranged according to a grade level or a collective of students can be invaluable in making an activity succeed.

SHORT-TERM THEMES

Title:	Webs, Organizers, Diagrams, and Shapes
Subject Areas:	Social Studies and English
Ages/Grades:	Grade 7, 8, or 9
Number of Students:	20 or more
Focus Points:	1. Representing information in various ways
	2. Using webs and graphic organizers in any area of study to focus thoughts and ideas
	3. Linking ideas in a consistent chain
Time Necessary:	2 days

OVERVIEW

Webs and graphic organizers are important tools in helping students access information and develop ideas into constructed patterns. These skills are particularly useful in mixed-ability classrooms because they may help students organize and present knowledge in flexible ways and while emphasizing clarity and depth. We have found concept webs and graphic organizers to be extremely well suited to cooperative classrooms in which students are creating and explaining information to peers.

Our theme in this activity is related directly to a skill rather than to specific content. The purpose is to give students a familiarity with different ways of organizing and displaying information. This is a skill that one student can use to make sense of a problem or to help another understand a concept. It is also a skill that falls under the concept of lifelong learning. Students who master these skills will be able to use them as tools with their own learning for their entire lives. Being able to construct a web or chart a diagram helps in a great many tasks associated with functioning in an environment where one has to translate information into problem-solving responses. These environments are found not only in school but in any aspect of life where problematic situations are encountered. The skills of creating these instructional aides also dramatically increase and reinforce understanding for those students who are primarily visual learners.

Often, educators look upon all skills as the province of one discipline or another. They are seen as being "owned" by a teacher or a subject area. Nothing is further from the truth. Although some skills are subject-specific, many others are interdisciplinary. This is particularly true at the seventh-, eighth-, and ninth-grade level, where the emphasis should be on providing students with the knowledge and tools necessary to master the more complex demands of learning they will encounter in the later years of education.

Our theme includes a number of styles of organizing thoughts and ideas. This is not to say that there are no other forms or that we have intentionally neglected one type or another. We have not. There are a great many ways of building graphic organizers and of using webs. The purpose of this unit is not

51

to list them all or to instruct teachers about using these various tools. The intent is to remind teachers that skills provide important interdisciplinary themes that can link the work of students and teachers.

INTERDISCIPLINARY OBJECTIVES

1. Students will be exposed to four forms of representing information graphically.

2. Students will demonstrate a mastery of two types of organizers, webs, or diagrams.

3. Students will become aware that they can invent their own diagrams or modify existing ones to fit their needs.

COMMON LINKAGES

Materials

1. Teacher-produced examples of webs, organizers, and diagrams

2. Student-generated materials

Activities and Time

1. Teachers, either working as team teachers in the same room or paralleling each other's work in separate classrooms, describe various ways of representing information and ideas. Teachers distribute sample webs, diagrams, and organizers. Teachers will split the material. This activity lasts most of the first day. Students are then asked to construct a web, organizer, or diagram for the next day based on a common example. This would be classified as a rough draft. Students are reminded that they are expected to do their individual best and to meet teacher-set standards, which include effort and breadth of understanding.

2. On the second day, students share their rough drafts in groups and look for creative comments. Students then begin a second graphic display for the next day's class.

3. Both webs, organizers, or diagrams are submitted to the teachers on the third day. Both teachers review what the students generate and return the student work later in the week with comments. Student work may be displayed and shared at a later date.

Factual Material

What constitutes a web, graphic organizer, or other diagram.

Skills

1. Building a web, graphic organizer, or other diagram

Concepts

1. The use of a web, graphic organizer, or other diagram to process, display, and organize information and ideas

2. The understanding that ideas or information representing knowledge do not necessarily have to be represented by writing or speaking

3. Development of one's own ways of organizing information and ideas

Assessment

1. Teacher assessment of student products

2. Student reaction and comment in reviewing the work of peers

Notes

This activity can be incorporated into a scope and sequence of skill mastery that can be developed by grade-level teachers or school communities. It is student-centered in that the individual success of each child is the overall aim. Students are not evaluated in comparison with peers but on the level of mastery they have reached. Following such a theme, teachers find themselves at the heart of a *teaming* relationship.

SHORT-TERM THEMES

Title:	Designing a Language
Subject Areas:	World History and English
Ages/Grades:	Grade 9
Number of Students:	20 or more
Focus Points:	**1.** The importance of a written language to a society
	2. Rules as the basis of languages
	3. How languages are reconstructed by people every day
Time Necessary:	1 week

OVERVIEW

During this one-week activity, students, working in groups, will design a written language. The language will have a set of symbols that carry meaning. Symbols may represent words or letters. Other symbols might be used to facilitate use of the language. Students may use whatever they design to represent components of their language. Their language also must have a set of at least five rules. Groups of students will be acquired to describe these rules and explain how they are used. Each group is also encouraged to produce at least one hands-on activity centered on its language in which the rest of the class can participate.

Designing a language can serve as an excellent introductory activity early in the school year. For example, during the month of September, World History classes might focus on the elements of culture within a civilization. Language is one of the key elements created by a culture. Similarly, for an English class about to embark on a study of our language for a school year, creating a language offers an opportunity to review the rules of language learned in junior high school and to use them in building a new language. This activity brings the often abstract idea of a language to the student and places it within the student's creative control.

To build a language and be true to actual language development, students must work in groups. The groups should be relatively large, with between six and eight members. This is a complex task that will require the efforts of all group members. It also is a social task that requires the interaction and exchange of a number of participants.

At the end of the week, students are expected to have a display or demonstration for the others in the class. Their displays can take the form of a museum in which the work of all groups is offered to others at the same time, or students may opt to present their material one group at a time. There are opportunities for adding new and different elements to the activity. For example, an additional component for the last day would have the teacher provide a long roll of paper covering a classroom wall, on which the groups display samples of their work.

INTERDISCIPLINARY OBJECTIVES

1. Students will demonstrate how rules are part of a language.

2. Students will see the link between language and civilization.

3. Students will design symbols with specific uses for a language.

COMMON LINKAGE

Materials

1. Teacher-generated examples of linguistic rules dealing with the English language

2. Teacher-provided examples of ancient languages

3. Student-generated activities

Activities and Time

1. As with other activities, students work on the activity during what would have been their social studies and English class periods. In a sense, they simply have a double period of time for the week. On the first day of the week, students are assigned to work groups and given an overview of the construction of the English language and the underlying logic. This should include group activities designed by the teacher. Day 1 also includes a teacher presentation about the languages of past civilizations. This also includes engaging students in group activities.

2. Days 2, 3, and 4 find students working on their group languages. Their final products should include visual displays and activities for other groups to try.

3. Day 5 is presentation day, when students share activities. Classrooms or a part of the school become activity areas or a museum. Students are also given a checklist sheet for assessing their group's work and the work of other groups. The last class activity finds students writing a description of and reaction to what they have been engaged in during the week. This is turned in at the next class meeting.

Factual Material

Elements and rules of the English language, basic elements and rules of languages from ancient civilizations (e.g., hieroglyphics)

Skills

1. Designing and using the rules of a language

2. Creating activities for other students

3. Developing group and collaborative skills

4. Conducting research

Concepts

1. Language is an essential component of civilization.

2. Language is based on a set of rules and has a developed organization.

3. Language means not only a standard language such as English or French, but also such areas as the language of music or math.

4. Language is a socially constructed entity.

Assessment

1. Student assessment of activity within their group

2. Student assessment of what other groups produce and demonstrate

3. Student-written narrative

4. Teacher assessment of group work

5. Teacher assessment of final student products

6. Teacher assessment of and reaction to student narratives

Notes

This theme-based activity can be extremely interesting for students as they become involved in constructing a final product that highlights their creativity and effort. Because this is an activity that might take place early in the year, teachers can help students select and develop roles within the group. Scheduling may become an issue. Teachers, administrators, and schedulers need to set up a time to allow teachers and students to come together. Although this activity is geared toward ninth graders, it can easily be adapted to a more complex study of language by a senior-level social science class and an English class. Likewise, this activity opens the door to greater interdisciplinary learning, as it could easily involve mathematics, foreign language, and science classes.

SHORT-TERM THEMES

Title:	Expanding a Fact
Subject Areas:	Social Studies and English
Ages/Grades:	Grades 7, 8, and 9
Number of Students:	20 or more
Focus Points:	1. Learning to identify a fact
	2. Writing based on factual information
Time Necessary:	1 day

OVERVIEW

The interdisciplinary theme of this activity focuses on a particular skill that is essential in all aspects of learning. Students are continually asked to read. Their reading is not limited to any one subject area. Often, after students have read a passage, a page, or a chapter, they are required to select a set of key points or to memorize information consisting of specific facts. Some students have mastered the complex skills involved in completing this type of activity, but others may not have done so.

The difficulty level increases when students are asked to write a summary narrative based on the researched facts. Students must first decide what is a fact and, second, select facts relevant to the topic of study. They must also translate the singular nature of a fact into written narrative description.

Summarizing is an important skill in itself, but it is not the final step in learning how to apply facts gained from critically reading certain material. Students should be able to take the facts, summarize them, and use them to form and support a personal opinion. This step demands more than a simple summary. It is one of the building blocks in framing an argument or a thesis. In our experience, students often do not master this sequence of skills in the early grades. Later, when they are required to produce a formal thesis, students may know how to find a fact and offer a summary but may still need practice at taking a fact and using it in their writing to expand and support their position.

It is in the seventh, eighth, or ninth grade that students should experience using and mastering these skills. Student weaknesses in this area should be identified, and strengths should be reinforced. The chain of skills suggested in this activity is clearly within the province of English and social studies teachers, who, working together to design a common scope and sequence of skills, can create a grade-level skills curriculum.

In this activity, lasting one day, students in English and social studies classes are presented with an overview of reading with a critical eye for facts. They are then arranged in groups of three and assigned passages to read. Groups identify a set number of facts and then collectively begin designing sentences to explain the facts. Groups are then assigned a thesis to follow and must use the facts to support points they create in a written narrative. At the end of the class, the groups share their products with others in the class and submit a written copy of their work. They are then assigned homework that repeats the classroom experience and is to be completed individually. This assignment is collected the next day.

INTERDISCIPLINARY OBJECTIVES

1. Students will master reading for facts.
2. Students will master using facts in a narrative summary.
3. Students will master using facts to support a thesis.

COMMON LINKAGES

Materials

1. Teacher-generated overview of the process (i.e., a graphic organizer)
2. Teacher-provided reading materials (not focusing on length)
3. Student products

Activities and Time

1. This is a one-day/one-class activity but should not be a once-in-a-school-year exercise. It must be repeated throughout the year by both teachers until skills are mastered. In one day, students can complete the steps of the activity: reading for facts, selecting facts, summarizing facts, and using facts to support a thesis. There is time for a teacher overview, although this becomes less time-consuming as the activity is repeated during the school year.

Factual Material

Definitions of a fact, summarizing, narrative, thesis

Skills

1. Critical reading
2. Writing a narrative summary
3. Identifying facts
4. Supporting a thesis
5. Developing group skills
6. Peer and self-editing

Concepts

1. The importance of using facts to support an argument
2. Using facts as a basis for developing writing

Assessment

1. Teacher assessment of group work and products

2. Teacher assessment of individual student skill mastery

Notes

This activity can and should be repeated at designated times during the school year. It does not demand any schedule modification, as the activity can take place in individual classrooms. It does demand that teachers work together in deciding what will be taught, when it will be taught (introduced and reinforced), and what constitutes mastery for individual students.

SHORT-TERM THEMES

Title:	Women of the Twentieth Century
Subject Areas:	World History, American Studies, and English
Ages/Grades:	Grades 9–12
Number of Students:	20
Focus Points:	1. Developing knowledge about biography and autobiography
	2. Learning about the contributions of women
Time Necessary:	2 weeks

OVERVIEW

At the center of this two-week activity are the dual topics of biography and autobiography, focused on the theme of women who have made major contributions to society. Although this activity can be incorporated into any unit dealing with historical overtones from grade 9 through grade 12, for purposes of discussion this section will focus on a twelfth-grade English class and United States History class. Students in groups of three select a biography or autobiography of a woman living during the twentieth century. If students choose a woman from another nation, they should note how she was viewed in the United States. Teachers furnish a list of possible topics, although students are free to make their own selection. Once a person has been selected for study, students read one book, either biography or autobiography, about that person. They also are required to conduct their own research into the person's background and to prepare their own biographical sketch.

The second week concludes with group presentations. These should include a twenty-page draft of the group's written analysis of the person's life, together with some additional demonstration component such as graphic displays, artifacts, or a dramatized video interview. All materials are geared toward presenting a better understanding of the woman selected by the group. Presentation may take two or three days, depending on the number of students involved in the class.

INTERDISCIPLINARY OBJECTIVES

1. Students will gain a greater appreciation of the role of women in the twentieth century.

2. Students will develop an awareness of the process involved in creating a biography.

3. Students will develop an understanding of how one must reconstruct reality in developing an autobiography.

4. Students will utilize group process and skills in completing the requirements of the activity.

COMMON LINKAGES

Materials

1. Teacher-generated materials
2. Student-generated materials
3. An autobiography or biography of a twentieth-century woman
4. Assorted research materials

Activities and Time

1. During the first four days, teachers present an overview detailing aspects of biographies and autobiographies. This presentation takes up a portion of the combined meeting time of each section. Students engaged in the activity meet during a double period for the two weeks.

2. During the first week, students, in groups of three, select the life of a woman to research. They begin a common reading of a biography or autobiography. As they read, they are encouraged to journal as writers, preparing to create biographies at a later point in the unit and thus creating their own realities in writing. They meet in groups to compare notes and begin their additional research into the topic.

3. The second week finds students completing their biographies or autobiographies. Students should also be at the completion stage of their research. By the second day of the week they should be engaged in writing their rough biography as a group. They should also begin to work on their presentations, due at the end of the week.

4. Day 3 of the second week finds students completing their presentations. The limited time available in a two-week activity demands that students do an equal if not greater amount of work outside of the scheduled class time.

5. Days 4 and 5 of the second week are devoted to viewing student presentations.

Factual Material

Women of the twentieth century, various historical events, autobiography, biography

Skills

1. Researching
2. Writing a biography
3. Preparing a demonstration
4. Organizing
5. Group process

Concepts

1. Understanding the use of a biography

2. Understanding the use of an autobiography

3. Women as significant contributors to the twentieth century

4. Biography and autobiography as a re-creation of a person's life

Assessment

1. Teacher assessment of group biography

2. Teacher assessment of group demonstration

3. Student assessment of other groups

4. Students' self-assessment

Notes

Although this activity involves a great deal of work and concentrated effort, it can be completed during a two-week period. A flexible schedule works to the advantage of both teacher and students. For example, a schedule that allows for a double block of time creates an almost ideal situation. Other schedule modification alternatives unique to each school may be possible.

As stated at the beginning of this section, an activity like this one can be used in any combination of social studies and English classes. Age and grade levels determine the topic, complexity, and outcomes. Regardless of grade level, the activity offers a unique opportunity for students to create their own interpretations of the life of a person and learn the process we use to re-create those lives. Students also create a knowledge base of the important roles women have played throughout history.

In addition to the wealth of biographies on twentieth-century women, Judith Bently's *Justice Sandra Day O'Connor,* Valjean McLenighan's *Women Who Dared,* Shyann Webb's *Selma, Lord, Selma: Girlhood Memories of the Civil Rights Days,* and, of course, Maya Angelou's *I Know Why the Caged Bird Sings* have all received high grades from students as well as appealing to a variety of interests and skill levels.

SHORT-TERM THEMES

Title: A Cookbook from Around the World

Subject Areas: Social Studies and English

Ages/Grades: Grade 7

Number of Students: 20 or more

Focus Points:
1. The connection between food and culture
2. The diversity of world cuisine
3. The importance of writing instructions clearly

Time Necessary: 3 days

OVERVIEW

The task of junior high school students engaged in descriptive writing and writing for directions takes on an added dimension when they use their talents to produce a document that can be shared with others. Students in social studies classes learning about various world cultures need hands-on activities coordinated with more traditional forms of classroom work that too often become standard classroom fare. This activity links the learning topics and efforts of two subject areas in a common theme that benefits all involved.

Working in groups of three, students conduct a day of research into meals from different cultural regions of the world or from a particular region under study. Their research takes up two class periods of the first day. During this time, students select a food that they wish to prepare. They draft a narrative of where the meal comes from, why it is popular, its history, and other pieces of information that fit in with an outline provided by teachers.

On the second day, students select ingredients and develop a recipe, including all the instructions necessary for creating their meal. Once they have finished their work, they produce a clear, formal, and readable recipe.

On day 3, students cook meals according to their recipes. Any adjustments are noted in the one-page narrative that accompanies each list of ingredients and cooking instructions. Students and teachers then enjoy sampling each group's meal. The edited recipes and narratives are compiled for a class cookbook.

INTERDISCIPLINARY OBJECTIVES

1. Improve students' descriptive writing skills.
2. Increase students' awareness of world cultures.
3. Demonstrate a respect for the diversity represented by various cultures.
4. Make students aware that they are responsible to others (the readers of the cookbook/the people tasting the meal).

COMMON LINKAGES

Materials

1. Research material about foods of the world
2. Teacher-supplied outline to assist in the development of narratives

Activities and Time

1. Groups are assigned. Students receive an overview about descriptive writing, complete with a teacher-supplied outline. In the second period of the day, students begin researching foods from another culture or region of the world.
2. Working in groups, students develop recipes and write the narrative. Proofreading and editing take place in groups. Roles are established for preparing food the next day.
3. Students cook their meal and bring their recipes to life. Additions are made to recipes and to narratives, which are then added to the cookbook. Teachers and students then sample the assortment of food. The cookbook is used to help the following year's class as they begin the exercise.

Factual Material

World cooking, descriptive writing, cultural regions of the world, recipes

Skills

1. Researching
2. Writing
3. Editing
4. Cooking
5. Collective group work

Concepts

1. The importance of culture
2. The diversity of cultures
3. The need for clarity in descriptive writing

Assessment

1. Teacher assessment of group recipe
2. Teacher assessment of group narrative
3. Teacher assessment of group and individual participation
4. Student assessment of activity (written homework assignment)

Notes

In three days, students combine work in two subject areas to produce a common product. The collaborative blending of class work that is an integral spinoff from the activity, as well as the production of a lasting document, a class cookbook, serves as an important example of what can be done. Seventh graders enjoy meeting expectations and watching the fruits of their labors become real.

As with other interdisciplinary work, the school librarian is a valuable resource who should be asked to become part of the teaching team. The library should be the source of descriptions of meals from around the world. Teachers may also request help in obtaining information about meals in other cultures from parents' organizations and from the larger community.

Learning to cook is a process of trial and error. Not all recipes will result in succulent creations or mouth-watering morsels. However, students whose meals do not tempt gourmets should be encouraged to correct their mistakes and try again, either during another activity or at home. Remember—the grade is for the effort and creativity, not the taste!

SHORT-TERM THEMES

Title: A Decade in a Century

Subject Areas: English, World History, and United States History

Ages/Grades: Grades 9–12

Number of Students: 20 or more

Focus Points:
1. The events that took place during a decade
2. The literature produced during a decade

Time Necessary: 2 weeks

OVERVIEW

The idea of a decade is a theme that offers benefits to both a social studies class and an English class. Again, the interdisciplinary exploration of the events and products of a ten-year span of history presents many opportunities for teachers to *team* and to *team-teach.* It allows students not only to focus consistently on the material from one discipline or another but also to use the work of another class to further their understanding.

To describe this activity, which can be applied at any of the high school grade levels, we select one decade to model, although there are innumerable options. Again, the teacher should decide which is chosen.

In this activity, an eleventh-grade American Studies class and an eleventh-grade English class focus on the decade of the 1920s. During this time, the English class reads *The Great Gatsby* or another work from the period. The American Studies class engages in a study of the decade. The two classes parallel each other, with a concluding exercise giving students a common planning time to work together.

Much of the content within each class remains as it would have without parallel teaching. Teachers remain in charge of designing their own curriculum during a two-week coverage period. Yet students have the opportunity to participate in two classrooms, each reinforcing the teaching of the other. Such an interdisciplinary activity only strengthens the learning process.

INTERDISCIPLINARY OBJECTIVES

1. Students will reach an understanding of the links between history and literature.

2. Students will develop a reading and analytic knowledge of a novel of the 1920s era.

3. Students will develop a historical knowledge of the 1920s and be able to relate the decade to earlier and later periods.

4. Students will continue to work on skills related to a critical understanding of the American novel.

5. Students will continue to work on skills related to constructing an in-depth understanding of a designated historical era.

66

COMMON LINKAGES

Materials

1. A novel such as *The Great Gatsby*

2. An American Studies text

3. Research materials provided in a school library

4. Teacher-generated material

5. Student-generated material

Activities and Time

1. Each class functions independently during the two-week period, except for the last day. It is desirable for students from the two classes to be matched or for more than one English teacher and more than one social studies teacher to participate. The English class spends the nine class days in a study of the novel. The American Studies class focuses on the events of the decade that surrounded the characters within the novel.

2. A final activity brings together all students engaged in the two classes. This activity could follow the lines of the Demonstration (Nowicki & Meehan, 1996), in which students might decide to enjoy the dances and music of the day while in costume. Many other alternatives could amplify and give focus to an event that brings closure to the theme and the topic. Students in groups of three are required to demonstrate one thing they have learned. This activity is not directed primarily toward assessment but, rather, toward enjoyment.

Factual Material

The events and people that made the 1920s a special decade, the characters and places associated with *The Great Gatsby*

Skills

1. Skills specific to each area of study (although many are similar)

2. Demonstration in a final exercise

Concepts

1. Literature that is grounded within a certain time and place

2. The complementarity of two disciplines on one area of study

3. The influence of existing conditions on an author and his work

Assessment

1. Assessment designed by the English teachers

2. Assessment designed by the social studies teachers

Notes

A two-week study such as this and an effort to come together at a common end point suggest that teaming can occur and that students can profit from being engaged in classes that complement each other. This is particularly true at the eleventh-grade level. The final activity need not be a means for assessment but should be a chance to connect the expertise from the two disciplines to benefit students. The time required is not an obstacle because students and teacher remain within their respective classes until the final day. Finding a block of time for a one-day activity is not too difficult once the barriers of separated disciplines have been opened.

SHORT-TERM THEMES

Title:	Folktales
Subject Areas:	American Studies, World History, English, World Cultures, and World Geography
Ages/Grades:	Grades 7–12
Number of Students:	20
Focus Points:	1. The folktale in relation to culture
	2. The folktale and fictional characters
	3. History and folktales
	4. Ethnicity and the folktale
Time Necessary:	3 days

OVERVIEW

Folktales, expressed in poem, story, and song, are a part of all cultures. Created by ordinary people and usually passed down in an oral tradition, folktales show us the heart of our common experience. Filled with vivid scenes and characters representing the best and worst in all of us, these stories speak of the whole range of human experience, from tragedy to comedy.

This activity focuses on the folktale and its relation to culture. It is applicable to any social studies area that deals with the culture a people share, either today or in the historical past. It is central to a study of any literary tradition because folktales are examples of the human experience, complete with sorrow, joy, desire, and fear.

Although folktales can be used within a number of course areas and at various grade levels, the example we offer is for eleventh graders studying English and American History. Students come together in an interdisciplinary setting to experience various nineteenth-century American folktales. Students not only read the tales but also spend a great deal of time listening to them.

The activity has three parts. The first begins with an overview presented by the teachers of what constitutes folktales and of the elements involved in their study. The teachers then present students with a list of folktales, which students working in groups will read. The teachers provide an information sheet containing 15 questions about the folktale and the historical period in which it developed, to be answered by the group.

In the second part of the activity, students are required to present the folktale or a shortened version of it to the rest of the class in a creative fashion.

The third part of the activity asks students individually to write a short folktale about an aspect of their lives in the 1990s. These are submitted to teachers for review or are shared with the class during an extra-day extension.

INTERDISCIPLINARY OBJECTIVES

1. Students will develop an awareness of folktales.

2. Students will identify the relationship of time, place, and population to the subject and content of folktales.

3. Students will identify the elements of a story that are common to folktales.

4. Students will attempt to write their own folktales.

5. Students will develop cooperative work skills.

COMMON LINKAGES

Materials

1. Folktales

2. Student-generated work

3. Teacher-generated work

Activities and Time

1. Teachers begin the activity, which brings two classes together in a double class period, with an overview of folktales. Also on this first day, students are assigned to groups of four. A list of folktales is distributed to the students, as is a worksheet containing at least 15 questions. The student work groups then select a folktale and, through research, complete the worksheet.

2. The second day finds students turning in their completed group worksheets and designing a demonstration for presenting their folktale to the rest of the class. They should be allowed to experiment and should be encouraged to be as creative as possible.

3. On the third day of the activity, students present their folktale to the rest of the class. They are then assigned the task of creating their own folktales, to be completed individually in a day or two. These folktales may be used to extend the activity for an additional day.

Factual Material

Folktales, periods of U.S. history, elements of a story and characterization, individual characters

Skills

1. Researching

2. Demonstrating knowledge of a folktale to others

3. Using cooperative work skills

4. Analyzing a story

5. Writing folktales

Concepts

1. The idea of a folktale as an important product of the language

2. The universal nature of folktales

3. Folktales as representations of historical and cultural diversity

Assessment

1. Teacher assessment of group worksheet

2. Student assessment of group process and cooperative work

3. Teacher assessment of group presentations

4. Teacher assessment of individually written folktales

5. Student reaction to folktale activity

Notes

This activity can serve as a short-term break from traditionally separated classes. It encourages interdisciplinary activity and can be applied to many classes and at any junior or senior high school grade. The idea of folktales is rooted in our culture, and examples abound. For this activity, teachers can select tales based on such people as Paul Bunyan, John Henry, or Pecos Bill.

An example of the importance of folktales as an art form is portrayed in a magnificent way by Julius Lester in his telling of *The Tales of Uncle Remus* and *More Tales of Uncle Remus.* These tales are a direct link with slave culture in the pre–Civil War South and the characters representative of elements found in many societies. Lester's additional work *Black Folktales* links the realities of African Americans with their African heritage. It is grounded in the experiences of African Americans in the United States. Though written in 1969, it is an excellent resource for a social studies class to use.

SHORT-TERM THEMES

Title: Who Was Julius Caesar?

Subject Areas: English and World History

Ages/Grades: Grade 9

Number of Students: 15–40

Focus Points:
1. Julius Caesar—Roman soldier, statesman, politician, and leader
2. Shakespeare's creation of Julius Caesar
3. Shakespeare's play *The Tragedy of Julius Caesar*
4. Separation of fact and fiction
5. Writers' use of poetic license

Time Necessary: 1–2 weeks

OVERVIEW

Julius Caesar was a powerful figure in the Roman Empire whose influence spread throughout the known world of his time. Today his name is still recognized and is synonymous with the Roman Empire. References to his existence are with us even today—for example, the name of the month of July. His assassination is generally recognized as the first of its kind. Our common knowledge of the events of his life and death have come to us not only from the study of history, but also because of the often performed Shakespearean play *The Tragedy of Julius Caesar*. Therefore, the question arises: "Who was Julius Caesar?" Was he the literary character who placed the people above himself: "What touches us shall be last served" (Act III, sc. i, 1.8). Or was he a shrewd politician who carefully calculated his rise to power?

This unit is designed for English and social studies classes to do a parallel study of this famous and influential Roman leader. It allows each class first to spend time working on subject-specific information, followed by interdisciplinary and cooperative work. The unit is designed primarily for two classes and does not require the same students to populate each class. This particular activity is actually designed for two classes with different students. It is important, however, that the time and place exist for the two classes to be combined for collaborative work.

This activity allows students to explore the factual and fictional Caesar to arrive at their own conclusions. In forging this definition of Caesar, students will cooperatively and individually explore themes of power, greed, ambition, corruption, military might, and the nature of government.

This unit also allows each teacher to structure activities around the interdisciplinary class time. This is important because the amount of time that each class will spend in preparing for the unit will differ. The English class will spend approximately one week reading the play and working with Elizabethan rhyme, meter, and vocabulary. Therefore, the planning and time sequencing of the interdisciplinary work are crucial to the success of the unit. Teachers, familiar with the needs and abilities of their respective classes, will be effective judges of the time each needs.

INTERDISCIPLINARY OBJECTIVES

1. Students will learn to separate fact from fiction.

2. Students will gain insight into the influence of rulers over a society.

3. Students will learn more about the daily life of another culture.

4. Students will work on critical reading skills.

5. Students will continue to refine cooperative work skills.

6. Students will develop comparison and contrast skills.

COMMON LINKAGES

Materials

1. Basic world history text

2. *The Tragedy of Julius Caesar* by William Shakespeare

3. Videos

4. Supplementary materials/readings prepared by the teacher

5. Additional material students uncover in their research

Activities and Time

1. Students in the World History class research the historical Caesar through their text, supplements, library materials, and videos. Students work on uncovering information about his character that will allow them to make inferences about the type of man he was. This material should be gathered in note form and transferred to timelines, charts, and organizers to present to small groups (3 to 4 days).

2. Students in the English class read the play. Generally, one act per night accompanied by a written summary is effective. Each day, students, operating in groups of three to four, compare summaries of the act and identify areas of difficulty requiring clarification (1 week).

3. After reading the play, students, still in their assigned work groups, analyze the literary Caesar. They concentrate on personality, character, ambitions, what he says, what others say about him, what he does and does not do. This material should be gathered in organizers and notes to share with the other class (2 days).

4. Students are grouped with members of the other class. For this type of activity, it is best to work in even numbers of two from each class, for work groups of four. Students share and compare information on the two Caesars and prepare organizers to present to the full class (1 day).

5. Students present information to the full class. If the combined classes number over 40, presentations need not be to all students at once. As

long as the comparison and contrast work groups are kept intact, the class can be separated into two equal-sized groups to make presentations more manageable (1 day).

6. For a final activity, students in each class write an essay answering the question, "Who was Julius Caesar?"

Factual Material

Elements of drama as necessary to read and discuss the play; facts, dates, and details about the life of Caesar and the Roman world at the time of Caesar's life.

Skills

1. Reading critically
2. Thinking critically
3. Making inferences
4. Sharing information
5. Working with comparison and contrast
6. Developing a note-taking style
7. Designing organizers and timelines
8. Separating fact and fiction

Concepts

1. Fiction as a way of learning history
2. Relationship of fact and fiction through author's poetic license
3. The corrupting effects of power
4. The objectivity of history, the subjectivity of literature
5. Dictatorship as a means of control

Assessment

1. Teacher evaluation of final written essay
2. Student and teacher assessment of mutually agreed-on goals
3. Teacher and student assessment of affective goals
4. Peer evaluation of presentations
5. Self- and peer evaluation of efforts within group work

Notes

This type of unit is an easy, manageable activity for those hesitant to try interdisciplinary work. It allows teachers to spend time in their own areas and to serve as consultants in their field of expertise as students struggle to com-

74

pare and contrast the two Caesars. Additionally, once the English students have truly grasped Caesar's identity, it is easier to return to the play for final analysis of themes or literary skills. The English teacher especially will note that students are quicker to reenter the play after the activities have expanded their knowledge of the man and the times. Now the discussion can center on dramatic elements, not on translating plot.

SHORT-TERM THEMES

Title:	Sport: Then and Now
Subject Areas:	World History and English
Ages/Grades:	Grade 9
Number of Students:	15–40
Focus Points:	1. Role of athletic competition in ancient Greece
	2. Types and forms of competition in the first Olympics
	3. Role of athletic competition in the contemporary United States
	4. Types and forms of athletic competition in the contemporary United States
Time Necessary:	1 week

OVERVIEW

Students in the two classes examine athletic competition as it existed two thousand years ago and as it exists today. During the activity, there is an opportunity for each class to work on subject-specific materials and to share the information and themes they discover with each other as students work toward refining their personal philosophy on cultural mores.

The world of sport is topic of constant fascination to students, especially high school students. Wherever they go in U.S. society today, they are bombarded by images of sports heroes selling merchandise. Media hyperbole for sports events saturates the airwaves, and metaphors of sport permeate our daily conversation. For some of our students, sports are the reason school exists. For others, sports are a waste of time and money. But whichever viewpoint students hold, this activity will engage them.

Timing of the event is flexible because most World History classes spend more than a few days on the Greeks, the design of their world, and their contributions to the modern world. The students need only come together for two days, which are the focal point of the unit. If the schedule does not allow this to occur, then teachers need to explore options for the classes to spend at least 90 minutes together for the activity to progress from the cooperative sharing of information and attitudes to the presentation of organizers.

This activity can be paralleled with any English class. If the school operates with electives on the ninth-grade level, it can be used in short story, creative writing, drama, poetry, or essay writing. The resources in English are plentiful and should satisfy all needs and levels.

INTERDISCIPLINARY OBJECTIVES

1. Students will learn to make connections between history and literature.
2. Students will continue to develop comparison and contrasting skills.
3. Students will develop insights into the mores of a culture.

76

4. Students will continue to work at developing and articulating a personal philosophy.

COMMON LINKAGES

Materials

1. World History text
2. English anthology
3. Assorted short stories, poems, and essays on sport
4. Student-generated charts, graphs, organizers
5. Videos

Activities and Time

1. Students in the history class research the early Greek Olympics. They examine location, specific events, rules, conduct, audience, participants, and rewards.
2. Students in the English class read various teacher-selected short stories, poems, and essays with a sports-oriented theme.
3. Two days are spent in each class preparing information to be presented to the other class on the role of athletic competition within their respective societies.
4. The two classes are brought together and students arranged in groups of four, two from each class. Students, using visuals and examples, report on their findings and take notes on the shared information. Students need one day to accomplish this portion of the activity.
5. On the second large group meeting day, students in each group share their findings with the large group for class discussion.
6. Students in each class individually prepare a final product that recognizes the reasons for societies to create athletic competition. Depending on the student and the teacher, there are a number of options—a personal essay, a short story, a poem, a song, a newspaper piece, or some other form to achieve this goal.

Factual Material

Olympics, Greece, dates, places, events, names, contests, teams, rules, and other material dealing with sports and the historical Olympics. In English the facts will be determined by the readings as well as critical reading and writing skills.

Skills

1. Researching a topic
2. Integrating research material into oral and written presentations

3. Creating charts and graphic organizers to present material

4. Delivering oral presentations

5. Refining comparison and contrasting skills

6. Constructing a personal philosophy

Concepts

1. Sports as a metaphor for society

2. Sports competitions as a reflection of society's values

3. Relationship of athletic participants to hero status

4. The need of human beings to compete against other humans.

Assessment

1. Peer evaluation

2. Student evaluation of mutually agreed-on goals

3. Teacher and student evaluation of group activities

4. Teacher evaluation of individuals' final products

Notes

This activity can easily be expanded into an actual Olympic Games in which the two classes represent opposing city-states and compete for the honor of their gods. With a few modifications, teachers can select three to four athletic events and competitors, and can include a literature element as each city-state must write an epic poem telling of its glories and must deliver an oral history of the city-state. Complete with costumes, this becomes a high-interest, enjoyable activity that demands organization, cooperation, and some social skills.

Although most schools have many resources for this unit, we recommend the anthology *Sport: Inside Out* edited by David L. Vanderwerken and Spencer K. Wertz (Texas Christian University Press, 1985) as a valuable source of poetry, short stories, essays, and critical commentary.

Additionally, there are possibilities for involving both math and science classes in the unit. Size and design of playing fields, measurements for events, biological reactions of the body under playing conditions, and trajectories of various spheres used in the games are just a few areas that involve these other disciplines.

SHORT-TERM THEMES

Title:	Declarations of Independence
Subject Areas:	American Studies, English
Ages/Grades:	Grades 10 and 11
Number of Students:	15–40
Focus Points:	1. Freedom from oppression and foreign interventions in a nation's affairs
	2. The variety of forms that declarations of independence can assume
	3. The many ways of defining *freedom*
Time Necessary:	2–3 weeks

OVERVIEW

In this activity, students work cooperatively to examine freedom in literature and the social sciences. In literature, there are countless pieces—from novels to short stories to poems and essays—that show the sacrifices people will suffer and the commitments they will make to gain freedom. In the earliest Greek myths, through the early English legend of Beowulf, continuing to the poetry of Shelley and Keats and to the wartime writings of Crane, Jarrett, Shara, and many others, the concept of freedom is a core element of human existence.

In social studies, human beings have grappled with the concept since the time of Moses, to the Roman slaves and Spartacus, through the dominance of absolute rulers, and continuing to the tyranny of oppression today. History has seen wars waged and governments made and toppled as people attempted to gain or deny freedom. Therefore, this is a theme worth examining from the perspectives of both English and social studies.

This unit is created as an advance organizer for both classes as the students create a personal definition of freedom founded on three readings. The very nature of the activity allows for the unit to be team taught or paralleled. Additionally, it is designed so that classes need never be brought together or can be joined and reconfigured at the very beginning. The ideal strategy, however, consists of three parts. The first and the third activity involve the two classes working together. The second activity would be subject-specific as well as interdisciplinary. We recommend joining the two classes and separating them into work groups of four, two from each class, for the first week's activities, to allow for a combination of different viewpoints.

After the first week, students return to their specific classes for the next part of the activity. In this segment, English students work with literature showing freedom, while history classes examine societies where freedom was a struggle.

The culminating activity is a one- to two-day event where students return to their original work groups and share their findings. These presentations can take various forms and employ different media.

Obviously, the ideal conduct of the activity requires a schedule that allows the two classes and their teachers to come together logistically. This is where the support of administrators is vital to the success of interdisciplinary unit building. Because this is not always possible once a school year is underway, we do offer alternatives. But it is imperative to restate our belief that schedules must be flexible enough to allow and encourage the type of sharing we model.

INTERDISCIPLINARY OBJECTIVES

1. Students will identify common beliefs about freedom.

2. Students will work at comparison and contrast skills.

3. Students will continue to develop cooperative working skills.

4. Students will develop a personal and societal definition of independence.

5. Students will continue to refine presentation skills.

6. Students will refine research skills.

COMMON LINKAGES

Materials

1. The United States Declaration of Independence

2. Ho Chi Minh's Democratic Republic of Vietnam's Declaration of Independence

3. Martin Luther King's "I Have a Dream" speech

4. Additional supplements supplied by teachers

5. Student-generated materials

6. Assorted novels

7. History text

Activities and Time

1. Students spend the first week studying, comparing, and contrasting the three declarations of independence. Students, ideally grouped with two members from each class, take notes, share insights and prepare organizers analyzing and comparing the three documents. After studying and discussing the nature of freedom, each student writes a two- to three-page paper forming his or her definition of freedom.

2. During the second week, students return to their subject-specific classes to work with their definitions of freedom.

   a. Students in English find a suitable number of short stories or poems that have freedom as a major theme. The exact number is mutually decided through teacher–student conference. Students analyze the pieces using the personal constructs of the previous week as the guideline. The English teacher may choose to supplement with any reading skill activities that he or she feels are necessary.

80

b. Students in the social studies class research an era, government, country, or city-state from the point of view of the types and degrees of freedom that the society demanded and the government allowed. They especially examine the tension within the society over issues of freedom.

3. During the third week, the students rejoin their collaborative work groups from week 1 to share their findings. Each student should have a formal presentation to share with the group.

4. The final segment of the activity occurs in the separate classes. English students create a short story or poem defining freedom; history students construct a framework for a free society. Time is determined by the individual teachers.

Factual Material

The three declarations of independence, societies, events, dates, people, characters, critical reading and writing skills as needed

Skills

1. Writing to persuade
2. Using nonfiction to influence ideas
3. Working cooperatively
4. Comparing and contrasting documents
5. Developing research and note-taking skills
6. Locating theme-appropriate material
7. Writing creatively
8. Preparing individual presentations
9. Sharing ideas
10. Identifying fact and fiction

Concepts

1. Freedom as a universal value
2. Relationship of literature to needs in a society
3. Freedom's personal nature
4. Freedom's societal nature
5. Literature as a reflection of universal truths

Assessment

1. Teacher and student assessment of mutually accepted goals
2. Student and teacher evaluation of affective goals

3. Student self-assessment

4. Peer evaluation of student achievement and effort

5. Teacher assessment of final product in each class

Notes

By looking at a single theme such as freedom from two different points of view and functions within the two disciplines, this activity truly involves students in their learning. Compartmentalizing themes encourages students to see themes as being owned by one area or the other. Even if there is overlapping, students see this as subject-specific rather than universal. Making students responsible for their learning with students from another area has a strong impact on their ability to generalize learning and understand that knowledge should not be broken into pieces with different disciplines owning different pieces. Learning becomes comprehensive and applicable.

SHORT-TERM THEMES

Title:	Historical Novels: Fact and Fiction
Subject Areas:	English, World Studies, American Studies
Ages/Grades:	Grades 8–12
Number of Students:	15–40
Focus Points:	**1.** Connections between fact and fiction
	2. Authors' use of poetic license
	3. Role of historical fiction
	4. Separating fact from fiction
Time Necessary:	3 weeks; 3–4 shared days

OVERVIEW

The focus of this activity is a historical novel set in the time period being studied in the history class. Teachers should carefully coordinate the era with the literature to ensure a sufficient number of historical novels for two classes. Ideally, if enough sets are present, students will choose from these offerings. This will allow for cooperative activity, with students grouped according to the novel each selects. Students should then be given time to complete the reading of the novel on their own. Students may be given subject-specific guidelines to follow. For teachers who use journals, however, we would suggest minimal journaling on this assignment or very concise and directed journaling. On occasion, students are overwhelmed by the journaling to the point that it dilutes the purpose of the close reading.

Once students have finished reading the novels by a predetermined date, students from each class are brought together for small-group discussion. Students from the two classes should be mixed into small work groups according to the novels they have read. The groups spend two days studying the novel. Students note historical events, dates, people, places, decisions, and statistics, as well as interpreting character, influence of setting, elements of plot, conflict, and theme. Through this discussion and activity, students verify factual materials and recognize the author's inclusion of fictional elements. As they work through this comparison and contrast, students begin to understand how fictionalizing events can bring certain facts alive. They also come to recognize the danger of accepting as truth the apparent factual elements an author might include. Further discussion should center on the role of the author and the author's right to use poetic license to create a story. In our experience, students become quite involved in defining the creative process and understanding the difference between a historian and a fictional writer.

The final part of the activity is again structured for students to apply and gain synthesis of what they have learned as each class works in producing a subject-specific product. Students then come together one more time to share these products in their group and with the full class or a portion of the combined class.

INTERDISCIPLINARY OBJECTIVES

1. Students will develop critical reading skills.

2. Students will learn to recognize fact and fiction.

3. Students will develop creative writing skills.

4. Students will develop cooperative work skills.

5. Students will understand the strong connections between historical fact and fiction.

6. Students will understand the use of historical fact to create fictional personae.

COMMON LINKAGES

Materials

1. History text

2. Supplementary resources supplied by teacher

3. Various historical novels

Activities and Time

1. Students in each class select a historical novel relevant to the period of history being studied. Students in the two classes are then grouped according to the novel being studied. Social studies students read the novel and verify the accuracy of the historical data in the novel. English students read the novel and concentrate on its genre and the literary devices the author employs to tell the story: plot, character, setting, theme, conflict, climax, denouement, and so on.

2. Following the gathering of the information as required in each class, students meet to discuss the novels in small groups. They concentrate on comparing and contrasting the historical facts and the author's additions and interpretations.

3. History students take a series of facts from the novel and write a newspaper account of the actual incident. English students create a short story or some other type of creative work from a series of facts about the historical incident.

4. The final day of the exercise is a general sharing and discussion of the students' pieces of writing.

Factual Material

Facts are determined by the selection of the historical incidents, events and characters. In English, the attention to facts is determined by the novel and by the students' critical reading skills and the literary devices employed by the author.

Skills

1. Critical reading
2. Comparison and contrast
3. Character analysis
4. Delineation of main events of plot
5. Verification of facts through research
6. Classification of information

Concepts

1. The factual basis of historic fiction
2. The influence on authors of events in society
3. The use of historic fiction as a way to increase student involvement
4. Understanding the use of historical fiction

Assessment

1. Student self-evaluation
2. Student and teacher evaluation of mutual goals
3. Peer evaluation of students' presentation and preparation
4. Teacher assessment of final product

Notes

Like many of the shorter interdisciplinary units we offer, this one is very flexible. It offers teachers time to work on achieving their own subject-specific goals while also paralleling the material in the other class. As a result, this strategy has a strong reinforcement component as students see similar themes being pursued in each area. Additionally, it gives teachers flexibility in scheduling common work time. Common time is also subject to change. Depending on the discussion and on student involvement, teachers can easily add a day or more if necessary. This activity can also be used for students to examine a popular television motif, the *docudrama*. Through this type of activity, students learn to view these television movies analytically. Consequently, the interpreting and discriminating thinking skills involved immediately become very useful and meaningful for students.

SHORT-TERM THEMES

Title:	Commitments
Subject Areas:	English, American Studies, World History
Ages/Grades:	Grades 9–12
Number of Students:	15–40
Focus Points:	1. Causes and effects of nationalism
	2. Effects of actions of countries on actions of individuals
	3. Role of government
	4. Individualism
	5. Role of choice within society
	6. Creation of personal values
Time Necessary:	2 weeks

OVERVIEW

This unit is designed for a situation where an English and social studies teacher share the same population of students, but in different class periods. Although the periods need not necessarily be blocked together, that would be helpful and a more efficient use of time. For the purpose of this model, we cite the American Civil War, but this study is applicable to many historical eras and need not be related only to war. It could work with the Industrial Revolution, the growth of cities in medieval days, the Renaissance, and a variety of other possibilities. It does require a block of approximately two weeks to give the activity the time to unfold to the final discussion of the videotape.

The activity has two distinct segments. The first segment is subject-specific, as students work on developing the foundation for the next week's activity within the parameter of each classroom. During the first week, the history students are involved in researching and examining the mood of the country in the period leading up the Civil War. They should look at the reason for legislation, economic structures, dependency, population, regional pride and nationalism, and growing dissent. While the students are studying this in history, in English they are reading short stories, poems, essays, and speeches that show the emotional issues of taking a stand. Both teachers should emphasize the unique effects of this war on people because it was a civil war, not nation against nation.

The second part of the strategy is the application phase of the knowledge. Students work during each class period as they prepare to examine the human impact of government's actions. The highlight is the preparation and production of a fifteen- to twenty-minute videotape comparing the causes of a war with the effects on individuals and families reacting to the event.

INTERDISCIPLINARY OBJECTIVES

1. Students will gain an understanding of the relationship of political actions to universal themes.

2. Students will learn more about the role of the individual within society.

3. Students will learn to evaluate moral and value judgments.

4. Students will continue to work on developing cooperative strategies.

5. Students will refine oral and written presentation skills.

6. Students will recognize the unique nature of the Civil War and the combatants.

COMMON LINKAGES

Materials

1. History text

2. English anthology

3. Supplementary materials prepared by teachers

4. Student-generated materials

5. Videos

Activities and Time

1. Students in the history class spend a week examining the emotional tenor of the country and the causes of the American Civil War. In completing this activity, students create various types of organizers to compare and contrast the causes from both Northern and Southern viewpoints.

2. Students in the English class spend a week reading materials written by people in conflict who face moral choices in times of war. Students will concentrate especially on characterization, theme, the choice, and the effect of the decision on the character and her or his family and friends. Students will complete theme and choice charts to compare the stories and other writings.

3. Using both English and social studies classes, students create a fifteen-to twenty-minute videotaped documentary (for a detailed description of the documentary, see Nowicki & Meehan, 1996). In this video, students examine the causes of war and the accompanying feelings of pride and nationalism. Through interviews with the literary characters, the documentary also reflects on the effect of the war and the individual moral choices characters had to make. Students will need approximately one week to script, rehearse, tape, view, and assess their efforts.

Factual Material

Causes of the American Civil War; people, places, events that were a part of the Civil War era. In English, the various characters and other facts associated with a short story or poetry study—characterization, setting, mood, tone, point of view, theme, conflict, and climax.

Skills

1. Reading critically
2. Identifying and classifying information
3. Recognizing literary devices used by an author
4. Writing analytically
5. Writing scripts
6. Role-playing literary and historical persona
7. Organizing time frames
8. Dividing work load
9. Creating costumes
10. Videotaping

Concepts

1. Relationship of personal commitment to action
2. Search for values
3. Human beings' willingness to sacrifice and suffer for morals and values
4. Literature as a record of people's struggle for truth
5. Nationalism

Assessment

1. Student and teacher evaluation of predetermined goals
2. Peer assessment of individual efforts and presentations
3. Student self-assessment of meeting affective goals
4. Teacher assessment of group activity and written materials
5. Student and teacher assessment of the final documentary.

Notes

The personal nature of this assignment becomes very important as it unfolds. Students become involved in the issues through their choices of literary and historical figures. The activity emphasizes the importance of students recognizing that there are consequences for actions and that these consequences are not always what was desired or imagined. Students can personalize the experience by examining their own moral and value code to write a short paper exploring at what point they would take a stand that might have negative or deeply moving and life-changing impact.

A valuable resource, if available, is Ambrose Bierce's *A Horseman in the Sky,* a powerful short story that quickly engages students in the activity as they realize the consequences of doing one's duty and sticking to a commitment. Many students have also become involved with the issues of war through reading Ray Bradbury's *Drummer Boy,* Robert E. Lee's "Letter to His Son," and Mary Chesnut's "Diary." Stephen Crane's *Red Badge of Courage* remains one of the best books on this theme.

SHORT-TERM THEMES

Title:	Oppression
Subject Areas:	English, American Studies, and World Studies
Ages/Grades:	Grades 9–12
Number of Students:	15–40
Focus Points:	1. The dual purpose spirituals served for Black slaves
	2. How spirituals reflected the connections of Blacks to Moses and the oppression of the Jews
	3. Spirituals as a blending of American religious practices and traditional African music
Time Necessary:	3 days

OVERVIEW

This unit is applicable to many different eras studied within the various secondary social studies and English classes. For the purpose of the model, however, we present the time frame of the early 1800s and the oppressed situation of the African-American people through enforced slavery.

Oppression of various peoples has always been and continues to be an unfortunate aspect of many societies. It is important for schools to target specific eras and governments that practiced such oppression so students can learn to identify the insidious ways it is used to demean and destroy a group.

This activity can fit into a number of places within the curriculum. It can serve as an advance organizer, an activator, a transition, or a summarizer to a unit on the role of African Americans and the slavery issue in the United States. It is not meant to be all-inclusive or comprehensive. Therefore the scope of the activity is tight; it is designed to be completed in two or three days.

The unifying motif for the two classes is the African American spiritual. Spirituals are a uniquely American form of music, which filled an important need for African Americans during the period of slavery in this country. A blend of American religious practice and traditional African music, the music connected the oppression of the slaves to the experiences of Moses and the Jews in the quest for the Promised Land. However, there were more subtle uses of the spiritual as a code to communicate routes to freedom and to share emotions that allowed the slaves to maintain their hope and dignity.

It is important that the two teachers involved in the study articulate carefully when and where the unit can be best utilized with their students. Once this is decided, the classes should be brought together and divided into groups of four, with two from each class. Students will analyze the spirituals, examine their symbolism, share and discuss their interpretations, listen to recorded spirituals or perhaps invite a local gospel group to entertain, and conclude by creating a modern spiritual about living under oppression today.

Following this collective experience, teachers have many options available for follow-up study. Again, individual teachers are the best judges and creators of curriculum.

INTERDISCIPLINARY OBJECTIVES

1. Students will learn cooperative work habits.

2. Students will develop a greater insight into the cultural past.

3. Students will develop an understanding of spirituals.

4. Students will learn to identify the elements of a spiritual.

5. Students will attempt to write their own spirituals.

6. Students will make connections from events of the past to events continuing today.

COMMON LINKAGES

Materials

1. Basic history text

2. English anthology

3. Books containing spirituals

4. Student-generated materials

Activities and Time

1. On day 1, students from each class are brought together and subdivided into groups of four, with two from each class. Students read and discuss the spirituals, examining both the historical perspective and literary elements such as repetition, meter, and rhyme.

2. On day 2, students share information and listen to recordings or a live presentation of the spirituals.

3. Working in small groups, students write and share spirituals that highlight oppression in today's world.

Factual Material

Spirituals, people, places, dates relevant to the plight of the African American and the songs, as well as literary devices such as repetition, refrain, meter, rhyme scheme, and symbolism

Skills

1. Recognizing rhyme scheme and meter

2. Working with symbolism

3. Making time connections

4. Writing spirituals

5. Sharing information

6. Recognizing era-specific material

Concepts

1. Literature that is produced in times of stress

2. Literature as a way of dealing with adversity

3. The human ability to find hope in times of despair

4. The human need for faith

5. Humans' indomitable will to persevere and survive

6. People's inhumanity to people

Assessment

1. Teacher and student evaluation of affective goals

2. Peer evaluation and assessment of information shared

3. Teacher and peer evaluation of methods of sharing information

4. Teacher assessment of final product

Notes

It is important to reinforce the adaptability of this strategy. Flexibility as to when and where to use this activity is one of its strongest attributes. Additionally, it is fun for students because of its activity-centered nature coupled with listening to and playing of the music. The ideal is to have a group come to the school who can play and discuss the music with the classes. Consequently, it can lead to discussion on the nature of faith and hope and the role these beliefs served and continue to serve in people's lives. To further bring the images to life, a picture book for all ages is the wonderful *Follow the Drinking Gourd* by J. Winter. It does a beautiful job of showing the derivation and utilitarian nature of the famous spiritual.

SHORT-TERM THEMES

Title:	The Search for Justice
Subject Areas:	English, Drama, and American Studies
Ages/Grades:	Grades 9–12
Number of Students:	15–40
Focus Points:	1. Theme of justice
	2. Jury system of trials
	3. Literature reflecting the attitudes of society
	4. Participation in a trial
	5. Role of choice within society
	6. Creation of personal values
Time Necessary:	Flexible—1 day–3 weeks

OVERVIEW

This unit requires only one day of shared interdisciplinary activity, although it demands approximately two weeks of lead time in each class to establish the parallel theme and prepare for the joint activity day. The history class must bring to the common activity an understanding of the jury system. Ideally, parallel instruction is used to study the role of African American society in the American culture of the 1930s in history class while an English class reads *To Kill a Mockingbird* by Harper Lee. Some time should be spent in each class discussing various meanings of *justice* and the operation of the criminal court system and jury trials.

The history class should analyze the period of the 1920s and the 1930s with respect to race relations in the southern United States. The emphasis should be on examining the issues of segregation, separation, integration, protest, rule breaking, and the effects of these issues on both whites and African Americans. While the history class is examining the turmoil and attitudes of southern race relations, the English class will be reading and studying *To Kill a Mockingbird*. Therefore, communication and planning time are necessary for the teachers to arrive at a certain point at a prearranged time.

After reading and discussing the novel, the English class will script the portion of the novel dealing with the trial scene of Tom Robinson. They will cast members of the class in specific roles, create a setting, design costumes, and prepare to videotape the trial scene. Once prepared, the English class will present its courtroom drama to the history class, who will serve as the jury. After hearing the case argued, the jury will decide the fate of Tom Robinson based on the information presented at the trial. Following the verdict, history students will write a paper explaining their vote.

INTERDISCIPLINARY OBJECTIVES

1. Students will refine cooperative work habits.

2. Students will develop an understanding of the jury system.

3. Students will learn that justice is not always perfect.

4. Students will attempt to identify weaknesses in the jury system.

5. Students will learn the difficulties involved in achieving justice.

6. Students will learn to increase their knowledge through role playing.

COMMON LINKAGES

Materials

1. *To Kill a Mockingbird* by Harper Lee

2. History text

3. Student-generated scripts

4. Supplementary materials supplied by teachers

5. Video of the Robert Wise film *To Kill a Mockingbird,* starring Gregory Peck

Activities and Time

1. Students receive copies of the novel *To Kill a Mockingbird* so that all students in the English class can complete the reading by a certain date.

2. During the first week of the strategy, students in the English class discuss the major themes and elements of the novel. They concentrate on setting, characters, history of the town, attitudes, and conflicts. At the same time, the students in the history class study race relations and the inequities of the pre–civil rights era. They concentrate on the causes and effects of segregation, the separateness of the two societies, and the stereotypes and prejudices that these beliefs fostered.

3. During the second week of the activity, the English class creates a script of the courtroom segment of the novel, when Tom Robinson is being tried for the rape of Mayella Ewell. Students attend to all areas involved in creating a play. They write dialogue, create the setting, establish background, design costumes, rehearse, and videotape the final presentation, scheduled for Friday of this week.

4. During the second week the history class examines case studies of African Americans on trial. They examine the alleged crime, motives, evidence, quality of legal defense, and justification for the sentence.

5. On Friday of the second week, the English class presents the courtroom drama for the history class, who serve as the jury. Once the jury votes, students individually prepare a two- to three-page paper justifying their vote and exploring the dynamics of the discussion of Tom's guilt or innocence in the jury room.

Factual Material

Specific facts, people, and places from the novel as well as facts brought out in the trial; additional information and facts about the criminal court system, such as the roles of jury, judge, bailiff, witnesses, prosecution, and defense attorney. Students in the history class will examine the events and people of the 1920s and 1930s, the early stages of the civil rights movement, and treatment of African Americans.

Skills

1. Developing listening skills

2. Writing scripts

3. Reading critically

4. Evaluating and analyzing information

5. Costuming

6. Role playing

7. Videotaping

8. Writing reactions

9. Justifying actions and beliefs

10. Analyzing case studies

Concepts

1. The idea of justice as a basis of the jury trial system

2. The search for justice as it is influenced by the prejudices of human beings

3. The relationship of truth to fairness

4. Differing standards of justice

Assessment

1. Student and teacher assessment of predetermined goals

2. Student self-assessment of effort and involvement

3. Peer evaluation of group activities and presentations

4. Student and teacher assessment of commitment to role and process

5. Teacher assessment of final written activity

Notes

As noted earlier, this activity can be either loosely or tightly structured along interdisciplinary lines. If time is a problem, then a minimum of one day can be set aside for the interdisciplinary aspect of the unit. If teachers' situations allow, however, there are a number of ways to expand on the combined activities. We offer this as a way of showing teachers that any beginning is a step in the right direction. Gradually, as teachers' confidence increases with the smaller pieces, the logical progression is to more complex and interrelated units. Additionally, if administrators object to or are unable to meet the needs of longer term interdisciplinary work, this is a step toward converting the nonbelievers, and it enables teachers to argue from an increasingly solid foundation for implementing schedule changes to foster this type of instruction.

SHORT-TERM THEMES

Title:	Playtime (Theatrically Speaking)
Subject Areas:	English, Drama, World Studies, and American Studies
Ages/Grades:	Grades 7–12
Number of Students:	20
Focus Points:	1. Background of a historical event
	2. Creating characterizations
	3. Writing dialogue
	4. Critical thinking
Time Necessary:	2–3 weeks

OVERVIEW

This activity is designed for an interdisciplinary unit in which, ideally, the English and social studies teachers would share the same students. Although it would certainly be a plus if the two classes were scheduled sequentially, that is not a prerequisite.

In this activity, students research a historical event with dramatic implications. A number of these exist, even within the same unit. Depending on class size, the students could be separated into two groups, with each group dramatizing a historical event. For example, in a unit on the Civil War, one dramatization might be the surrender at Appomattox; another might be Lincoln's arrival, tour, and speech at the Gettysburg cemetery; and a third might be Lincoln's assassination. For the Middle Ages, students might dramatize the signing of the Magna Carta or a discussion of the effects of the Black Plague and ways to combat the disease. There are a number of examples in popular media that teachers can use as examples to stimulate students' interest.

This activity appeals to students in a number of ways. It contains three primary segments: (1) research, (2) script writing, and (3) dramatizing. Once involved, students have the opportunity to create characters, put words in their mouths, and use poetic license through additional characters and various elements of plot.

For teachers, this is a powerful interdisciplinary activity that allows each teacher to emphasize subject-specific materials for the first week of the activity, then be the coach on the sidelines as the students put their learning to work by combining elements of both classes. Therein lies the strength of this unit. Although the strategy could be conducted in only one discipline, it would lack the depth of research or the insights into dramatization. By using both English and history, it offers so much more to the students involved.

INTERDISCIPLINARY OBJECTIVES

1. Students will recognize historical events as a basis for literature.

2. Students will learn to identify important facts about an event.

3. Students will identify and work with elements of drama.

4. Students will learn the process of writing a play based on historical documentation.

5. Students will come to an understanding of historical knowledge of a specific era or event.

COMMON LINKAGES

Materials

1. History textbook

2. English drama text

3. Supplementary materials prepared by the teacher

4. Supplementary materials prepared by students

5. The student-written plays

6. The videotape of the final presentation

Activities and Time

1. During the first week, students in English class work on identifying, recognizing, and using the elements of drama such as staging, blocking, characterization, suspense, dialogue, symbolism, and developing character through dialogue as well as action.

2. During the first week in history class, students identify the event and conduct their research. Students might be grouped according to tasks, such as people—who? why? personality? purpose? Another group might investigate the causes leading up to the event. A third group would investigate the effects of the event both on the participants and on the society. A fourth group would examine setting and create maps, charts, and timelines. As the week progresses, students would share information as a full picture of the event unfolds.

3. During the second week, the students work on scripting the play during both classes. Using the historical research, students create personalities for the people; construct scenery to represent the setting; work on including causes, reasons, and motivations into the script; and create dialogue as necessary to put the event into a historical framework, possibly by adding additional fictional characters. Finally, the group polishes the script and prepares for presentation.

4. The presentation is held during the third week. Other classes might be used as an audience, or, if created in a high school class, the drama could be presented to a middle or elementary school audience. In this way, the end product would model interdisciplinary learning for other students and teachers as well as serving as a powerful instructional tool for younger students.

Factual Material

In addition to the elements of drama, all people, events, places, dates, and other information students discover and use as a result of their research

Skills

1. Writing a play
2. Conducting research
3. Creating historical personae
4. Blending historical fact into a story line
5. Extending creativity and imagination
6. Costuming
7. Visualizing a setting through research
8. Videotaping
9. Using inferential thinking skills
10. Acting
11. Directing

Concepts

1. The relationship of literature to history
2. Historical events as a basis of drama
3. Presenting knowledge of historical facts in many forms
4. Understanding drama as a genre of literature

Assessment

1. Student and teacher assessment of predetermined goals
2. Peer assessment of group efforts and achievements
3. Self-assessment of accomplishment of affective goals
4. Student and teacher evaluation of the depth, seriousness, creativity, accuracy, and impact of the final presentation

Notes

This activity can truly be a team teaching effort. Although each teacher works individually with each class for the first week, in the second week the teachers function on the highest level of teaching, acting as "coaches" for the "team" of students who are producing a final product. This is an example of teachers sharing knowledge and sustaining the acquisition of knowledge by knowing when to step back and let the students become empowered to control learning.

In searching for resources, do not overlook some very well done television dramas, such as Michael Braude's *Gettysburg,* or Glenn Jordan's production of *The Court Martial of George Armstrong Custer* starring James Olson. Both are well done and involve students in realistic themes.

SHORT-TERM THEMES

Title: The Author Writes . . .

Subject Areas: English, American Studies, and World Studies

Ages/Grades: Grades 7–12

Number of Students: 15–20

Focus Points:
1. How literature reflects the society in which it is produced
2. Using inferential thinking activities to create a foundation for further critical analysis
3. Using themes to relate to history

Time Necessary: 1 week

OVERVIEW

This activity is designed to serve as a form of advance organizer as students use literature to draw inferences about the history of the society they are studying. Although there are similarities in this activity to other strategies, the difference is that only the literature is studied for the agreed upon period of time. No historical research or historical textbooks can be used. The ideal would be a team teaching situation in which one class of students functions with the two teachers, but it is adaptable to other situations. The most suitable alternative would be two teachers sharing the same class population, but meeting in different time blocks. Regardless of the logistics, the role of teachers would remain the same. Each teacher serves as a resource person available to question and guide students through a series of inferential skill-developing activities that will strengthen students' critical thinking skills.

It is very important for the two teachers to have time to plan this activity. The teachers need to select the materials for the study carefully and list the skills and assessment procedures that will form the foundation of the activity. The timing of the unit is critical to its success. It should occur at a point in the year at which students have gained a number of skills through analysis and close reading of literature and history. Students need to have at least a cursory understanding of the connections between literature and history. Additionally, they need to have a foundation of skills for working cooperatively.

It is crucial to the success of this activity that history teachers reinforce ideas such as forming and testing historical hypotheses; discovering, interpreting, and analyzing artifacts as a means of dating a civilization or culture; and the continued importance of recognizing cause and effect in determining the direction of history.

As for the subject matter, we recommend that teachers carefully choose from different literary genres to capture an effective overview from which students will work. Included should be a short story, a number of poems, an opinion essay, and possibly some other descriptive or mood piece. Each piece of material selected should have a clear relationship to the times that produced it.

100

During the week's study, the class periods will be devoted to reading and interpreting the work. The English teacher will assist with working through areas such as plot, character, setting, conflict, climax, symbol, figurative language, and point of view. The history teacher will help maintain a historical researcher's focus, reinforce interpretation of artifacts, review elements of culture, and stress the importance of students remaining unbiased observers.

INTERDISCIPLINARY OBJECTIVES

1. Students will continue to emphasize cooperative work habits.

2. Students will share information.

3. Students will develop an understanding of an era through its literature.

4. Students will continue to learn of the relationship between literature and history.

5. Students will recognize the importance of drawing inferences as a part of research.

6. Students will continue to develop critical reading skills in the various genres of literature.

COMMON LINKAGES

Materials

1. English anthology

2. Supplementary materials supplied by teachers

3. Student-generated materials and presentations

Activities and Time

1. Each day during the week will be devoted to a specific reading and analytic discussion. For these purposes, students will be assigned to discussion groups, which will continue to function throughout the week. Approximately ten minutes should be set aside at the end of the class each day for quick reports to the full class. As the week progresses, students should develop organizers highlighting the elements that tell about the era. Among these should be historical hypotheses and artifacts, as well as a completed chart documenting themes, attitudes, events, people, settings, causes, and effects. The final day will consist of group presentations of what they have uncovered as literary artifact hunters. Each student will then complete a two- to three-page paper in which they personally construct, through their inferential conclusions, the historical events or era.

2. Students are now ready to begin the historical study of the era with this foundation of information and understandings to direct them.

Factual Material

This will be determined by the selection of the materials for the class to study. Included should be people, authors, dates, settings, events, points of view, characters, and elements of the various genres.

Skills

1. Drawing inferences

2. Reading critically

3. Working cooperatively

4. Developing organizers and graphs to display information

5. Researching literary artifacts

6. Presenting orally

7. Writing a summary

8. Coming to conclusions

Concepts

1. Literature as a reflection of history
2. The influence on authors of their surroundings
3. The idea that knowledge is universal, not compartmental

Assessment

1. Student and teacher assessment of predetermined goals

2. Student self-assessment of achieving affective goals

3. Peer assessment of cooperative work skills

4. Teacher evaluation of oral presentations

5. Teacher assessment of written paper

Notes

This activity not only stresses interdisciplinary work but further emphasizes the critical skills of putting pieces together to form a big picture. As this occurs, students begin to see the importance of cause and effect and the relationships between the various elements of a society. As students next begin an in-depth study through the history class, the connections have already been made and the history teacher's emphasis can be tightly circumscribed without trying to shotgun all the peripheral yet important material. The reinforcement nature of this activity continues to grow throughout the history component.

SHORT-TERM THEMES

Title: The School's the Place

Subject Areas: English, American Studies, World Studies, and Social Sciences such as Sociology, Anthropology, and Political Science

Ages/Grades: Grades 8–12

Number of Students: 15–40

Focus Points:
1. The connections between students' lives, the creation of literature and history
2. Students as historians
3. Students as creators of literature
4. Students as researchers

Time Necessary: 4–5 weeks

OVERVIEW

This strategy taps into the students' own world and provides a foundation for a study of history and language arts as they study their own school to prepare a documentary and anthology. Although we see it primarily as a summarizing activity for students who have mastered certain skills and developed a realm of knowledge to use in the activity, it could be adapted as a way of teaching those skills at the beginning of a year. The model we offer is for a situation in which the English and social studies teachers share the same population of students in two different class periods. Although the periods do not have to be blocked together for it to work, this would certainly save time and facilitate the activity.

In this unit, students use their school as the society to be studied. If the school has been in existence for many years, teachers may want to separate the study into eras for manageability. However, the study of the school as a society covers all areas of historical research. There is a timeline, a map of its territory, its heritage, its people and leaders, its influence, effects on it of wars and societal conflicts, its folklore, its legends and heroes, its economy, its struggles through times of prosperity and times of austerity, its physical changes and improvements, its ethnic foundations and population shifts. It's all there waiting for the students to uncover the past and put it in perspective.

Additionally, records abound on schools for researchers to uncover. Many schools maintain previous student newspapers, yearbooks, and athletic records, as well as lists of graduating students. Local newspapers provide a wealth of information in researching past records and events because of the importance of the school to the community. People in the community, from retired teachers and other staff members to long-time residents who are graduates of the school are valuable primary sources waiting to be studied.

Once material is uncovered, the English focus begins. There are a number of ways to chronicle this history. It can serve as the basis for term papers, newspaper writing, journaling, short stories, poetry, songs, descriptive writing, expository writing, and so on.

Obviously, this activity demands a high degree of teacher preparation and coordination. Teachers must have a clear picture of specific skills, facts, and concepts for students to acquire through this study. They must carefully list subject-specific areas and the interdisciplinary involvement desired. The final documentary and anthology must be clearly planned and carefully coordinated.

INTERDISCIPLINARY OBJECTIVES

1. Students will understand the importance of the linkages between the social sciences and language arts.

2. Students will understand that history is alive and personal.

3. Students will learn to interview and create primary sources.

4. Students will recognize the relationship between their world and the larger society.

5. Students will prepare an anthology of short stories, poems, songs, essays, narratives, and interviews.

6. Students will prepare a videotaped documentary of the history of the school.

7. Students will understand how today's reality is built on the multiple realities of the past.

COMMON LINKAGES

Materials

1. Local newspapers

2. School-generated materials such as yearbooks and school newspapers

3. Various school records

4. Student-generated materials through interviews

5. Additional supplementary material uncovered by student researchers.

Activities and Time

1. Week 1: Teachers in each class will review the skills necessary for the researching and documenting material. Students will be assigned to work groups, and various topics will be generated by the class.

2. Week 2: Students will begin researching, organizing, and filing their findings for later presentations. Students should be identifying possible new sources, interviewing them, and transcribing the interviews.

3. Week 3: Students should now be moving ahead with the results of their findings. Timelines, maps, population demographic charts, graphs, and organizers should be under construction. Additionally students should be conceptualizing the anthology and documentary.

4. Week 4: Research should be completed and students should now be putting it together. Teams should be assigned to the major projects, the anthology and the documentary. These can be assigned by subject, the documentary for social studies and the anthology for English, or a combination. Outlines and materials for each project should be in progress.

5. Week 5: Scripts should be written, graphics prepared, and sequence established for the documentary. Short stories, op-ed pieces, essays, poems, interviews, and narratives should be in the editing stage for the anthology.

6. Week 6: Rehearse and videotape the documentary; publish the anthology. Both of the final presentations should be shared throughout the school and the community. One way to highlight the students' work is to hold an open house, complete with various exhibits and displays and culminating with watching the video.

Factual Material

For the most part, other than knowledge of the skills involved, this would be material uncovered by the students in the process of their research.

Skills

1. Writing essays, poems, short stories, and journals
2. Interviewing strategies and transcribing
3. Organizing time and materials
4. Classifying information
5. Working cooperatively
6. Researching
7. Taking notes
8. Preparing charts, graphs, timelines, and organizers
9. Videotaping
10. Scripting
11. Being responsible
12. Keyboarding

Concepts

1. Literature as a reflection of the social environment
2. How history is created by people everywhere
3. The idea that the more local the subject matter, the greater the imprinting
4. The idea of the school as subject matter for history and language arts

Assessment

1. Teacher and student assessment of predetermined goals
2. Teacher and student assessment of mutually acceptable affective goals
3. Weekly teacher checklist of student progress
4. Teacher assessment of students' weekly progress journals
5. Self-assessment of group efforts and accomplishments
6. Teacher assessment of final products

Notes

Part of the fun of this activity is that students know they are creating products that will be viewed and assessed by community members and will become a part of the permanent archives of the school. This type of accountability and notoriety has a strong influence on involving students in the activities. They are examining materials with which they have some knowledge and insight. Another way of presenting material could be a "Then and Now" display highlighting various eras in the school's past compared to the present population of the school. Additionally, there are a number of ways for other disciplines within the school to become involved. However, ultimately students are the researchers, writers, and directors of a large-scale product that reinforces skills and uses accumulated knowledge to expand and broaden their world.

A drawback could be a curriculum lacking the flexibility of allowing history to live and literature to record it. The issue of coverage versus equipping students with a foundation to function at a higher level of thinking and cooperating is a continuing area of controversy and discussion. Yet we believe students must have a voice and an opportunity to expand that voice through their involvement, not through memorization and recitation.

CHAPTER 4

Unit-Length Interdisciplinary Themes

"You know, everything we did was centered around English and social studies. We team taught everything for a full year in a double block of time. It got so good that we could teach other's lessons. I guess we learned a lot from each other, too."

Mrs. "H"

INTRODUCTION

This chapter presents six strategies for term-length interdisciplinary thematic units for English and social studies teachers. As with the previous chapter, these themes highlight subject-specific areas as well as interdisciplinary linkages to stimulate broader based learning. These strategies are especially designed for teachers who, with willing colleagues, feel confident in plunging ahead to link their English and social studies classes. In this regard, these thematic and interdisciplinary strategies are meant to serve as prototypes for teachers to follow as they construct their own linkages across the curriculum. Teachers need the freedom to modify, to expand, and to spin off their work to meet the needs of the students in their school communities. Our strategies can provide a sense of direction for teachers and administrators as they reshape the way learning is organized and pursued within their schools.

On a different level, these interdisciplinary and thematic strategies offer teachers direct access to materials, activities, and lesson designs that they may use immediately. To help teachers structure the unit, we include a listing of interdisciplinary linkages between English and social studies, guides to parallel themes in each class, subject-specific information, and interdisciplinary activities to engage both classes in common learning and knowledge acquisition. We also outline assessment criteria that involve students in the process of evaluating effort, involvement, attitudes, fact and skill mastery, and conceptual development.

We realize that many teachers are operating in rigid structures and organizations that prevent cross-disciplinary activity in a full team-teaching or shared-student situation. To help those teachers, the strategies in this chapter either allow for those logistics or are adaptable for teachers to use in teaming relationships that parallel each others' work.

We believe that these activities offer teachers a window of opportunity to come together in a professional dialogue to share their ideas and expertise. In this way, teachers will become truly empowered to direct student learning in a more socially responsive and relevant manner.

UNIT-LENGTH THEMES

Title:	A New World—A New Literature
Subject Areas:	English and Social Studies
Ages/Grades:	Grade 10
Number of Students:	40–45
Focus Points:	1. America's coming of age
	2. Revolution
	3. Forming a new government
	4. Growth of the country
	5. America finding a voice
	6. The birth of American literature
Time Necessary:	Approximately 9–10 weeks

OVERVIEW

The period from 1750 to 1820 saw tremendous change in the New World as a transformation occurred from a colonial society dependent on Great Britain to an independent nation struggling to implement a democracy that would "form a more perfect union." As dramatic as the changes were in government, literary developments kept pace and evolved from utilitarian literature to an emerging American voice, truly unique and separate from European writings.

In the early days of colonial dissent triggered by England's treatment of the colonies, the literature reflected the tenor of the themes in the fiery rhetoric of Patrick Henry and Thomas Paine. As the upheaval continued, the literature and writing remained parallel to the era's events through pamphleteering and persuasive oratory leading to the writing of the Declaration of Independence. Then, following the war as America achieved its independence and struggled for definition, the literature of Irving, Bryant, and Cooper epitomized the emerging American culture through the rise of national pride, character, and the American form of Romantic writing. Consequently, this unit can be a treasure chest of material for parallel teaching and teaming for certain common activities that reinforce and add greater depth to the issues, attitudes, and themes emerging as the nation takes shape.

This unit offers a strategy for linking the work of the language arts study of early American literature and the historical events chronicling the birth of the nation in the American Studies class. The 9- to 10-week program we offer describes activities, themes, and events that lend themselves to parallel teaching and teaming through a series of interdisciplinary activities that reflect the common interests of the students.

This activity does place demands on the teachers to involve students in the activity and to schedule for certain large-group interdisciplinary activities. Ideally, the social studies and English classes should be blocked together in the schedule, with one class following the other and the same students assigned to each class. For true sharing to be created as well as the opportunity for impromptu activities to grow out of the class sessions, there need to be concessions in building a schedule. However, even if that is impossible, opportunities for sharing must be present. Significant teacher preparation and planning are needed to deal with the logistics of having the students meet together at certain times. It is especially crucial to the success of the constitutional convention that students meet for an extended period of time so the activity can unfold at a natural and progressive pace. If that cannot be achieved, the unit loses impact and continuity.

Although we list five activities that require large-group functioning, there are a number of other areas for small groups that parallel and easily lend themselves to working together. Examples are obvious in the Revolutionary War and novel unit, as well as during the study of the Constitution and the comparable themes in literature. These options are as plentiful as the creativity of the teachers and students.

As with the other models, we list the facts, skills, and concepts for each discipline as well as the interdisciplinary concepts. These are meant as guidelines; they can and should be adaptable to the needs and demands of the class involved, but the nature of the activities must remain student-centered and heterogeneous. The activities we offer are created to involve all students in developing knowledge and using that acquired knowledge to form the foundations of personal constructs that will allow continued growth and development. Additionally, the heterogeneous activities stimulate students to a higher level of achievement through a personal stake in the products and in the results. When assessment and evaluation become part of a community rather than isolated and totally individualistic, all participants have a higher stake in the results.

INTERDISCIPLINARY OBJECTIVES

1. Students will develop an appreciation of the connections between literature and social studies.

2. Students will work with cause-and-effect relationships.

3. Students will recognize the importance of chronology in a growing process.

4. Students will refine cooperative work skills.

5. Students will learn to research, evaluate, and integrate source material into oral and written presentations.

6. Students will continue to hone their presentation skills.

7. Students will develop a greater understanding of American culture.

INTRODUCTION

This unit, designed to last 9 to 10 weeks, is created for teachers who wish to develop interdisciplinary linkages between American history and American literature. The unit meets three needs. First, it offers teachers activities with both classes operating together. Next, it offers parallel teaching opportunities where what is happening in one class has a direct influence on the other class. Finally, it provides time for each teacher to prepare subject-specific activities that best meet the individual needs of each discipline.

The strategies are such that the basic resources found in most departments and libraries should provide sufficient supplementary resources. As in other activities, we offer a timeline to guide teachers in specific segments of the unit. This series of deadlines is flexible, depending on the needs and priorities of teachers; however, we have found that including enough time for the specific activities is helpful for teachers who must meet the needs of a specific curriculum. Additionally, a time frame is important when two teachers are working together and activities are involved. If we did not heed the demands of time, the unit could fail for logistical reasons that can be addressed by creating a schedule.

THE ENGLISH CLASS FOCUS

Materials

1. Basic American literature anthology

2. Selection of novels

3. Student-generated materials

4. Library resources

5. Teacher-prepared supplementary materials

6. Videos

Activities and Time

1. Students begin the unit with an advance organizer, which lasts for two days. Students will examine and discuss pictures, posters, images, and other materials presented by the teacher about contemporary American life, followed by small-group brainstorming and classifying information about American society. Students will post, share, and discuss the efforts of their activity. They will write a one- to two-page paper answering the question, "What is an American?" These papers are shared and discussed on the second day and are posted for future reference.

2. Ben Franklin rounds out the week as students spend three days studying the man, his works, and his impact on colonial society. Students will create organizers and charts to present information about Franklin's writings and contributions. They will write a portion of their autobiography in the style of Franklin and, in small work groups, create three to four aphorisms for *Poor Richard's Almanac*.

3. Weeks 2 and 3 deal with events, writings, and attitudes in American colonies leading to the Revolutionary War. For these two weeks, the activities must be closely coordinated between the two classes. During week 2, students read and analyze the works of Crevecoeur, Thomas Paine, and Patrick Henry. Students work in small groups as they prepare two organizers. The first compares and contrasts the content and theme of each passage; the second examines the style, tone, and literary devices

used. Based on their work in American studies, their essays on "What it means to be an American," and the readings, students write a two- to three-page essay, again exploring the theme of what it means to be an American, but this time from the point of view of a citizen of the colonies facing the mounting problems with Great Britain.

4. During week 3, students in English analyze the Declaration of Independence. Working in small groups, they examine its content, style, point of view, and various literary devices such as repetition, parallelism, restatement, and rhetorical questioning. On the fourth day of the week, students in class select historical and time-appropriate roles and prepare for a debate. The proposition to be debated is whether or not the characters they have created will sign the document.

5. Weeks 4 and 5 are dedicated to novel study. Students select a novel set during the time of the American Revolution; a number of selections available are applicable to all reading levels. Distribution and selection of the novels should allow students to complete the reading before the week's activities begin. Activities should be structured so that each day is spent in examining aspects of the novel common to the period of the revolution. Such things as setting, influences, conflicts, parallel events, daily life, and common historical characters and places should be covered first. Then various activities should be planned to examine elements of the novel such as character development, secondary characters, plot, climax, foreshadowing, suspense building, and conflict, as well as some time on vocabulary study. For a final activity, students, working singly or in small groups, should develop a presentation for the entire class demonstrating key events, themes, and attitudes. Following is a possible (but by no means a comprehensive) list of activities.

   a. Students who have read the same novel role-play a major event or depict a major value or theme.

   b. Students write a chapter to continue the story.

   c. Students stage a debate between characters representing different viewpoints in different books.

   d. Students draw a comic strip of five to ten panels depicting the climactic event of the novel.

6. During weeks 6 and 7, students examine works of Washington Irving, William Cullen Bryant, and James Fenimore Cooper to determine the beginning of the American voice in literature as well as the emerging concept of romanticism. The class is divided into three groups, and each group is assigned a folktale by Washington Irving. After reading the tale, students are reassigned into groups of three, with each member representing a different tale. Students then examine and compare common themes and elements to build gradually a foundation for defining American Romanticism. Following the discussion, students compare the definition they have devised with a researched definition. Students then write a two- to three-page analysis of a different Irving folktale.

112

Next, the students will read "Thanatopsis" by Bryant. As advance organizer for this study, students briefly write journal entries about their thoughts on death and where they would like to be buried. It sounds morbid, but students love it. After small-group analysis and graphic organizing of the key elements of the poem, students write a poem about death following the Romantic model of Bryant.

The final activity in this section should examine the first American hero of literature and the relationship between the characters. Following discussion, students should compare and contrast how the model established by Cooper in his *Leatherstocking Tales* for his hero, Natty Bumppo, and sidekick, Chingachgook, is portrayed in popular fiction and the media today.

7. For this week, the classes are again brought together for the week-long activity of a constitutional convention. As history students role-play the constitutional convention of 1787, the members of the English class document the proceedings, conduct interviews, prepare news stories, write op-ed pieces, design editorial cartoons, devise advertisements, and write feature stories of the characters and events. The week's events culminate in a weekly newspaper of the convention.

8. For the final activity of the unit, English students read, discuss, analyze, and work with literature based on an issue of freedom or government as documented in the constitution. Possibilities include the study of short stories, poems, essays, plays, and excerpts from longer pieces that show the struggles of society to maintain and preserve the freedoms and the structures of that great document and the Bill of Rights.

This portion of the unit lasts one to two weeks and concludes as the American studies class discusses the Bill of Rights.

Factual Material

Elements of literature such as foreshadowing, setting, plot, theme, suspense, characterization, stereotyping; genres such as folktales and legends; additionally, characters, authors, background data, and historical events that influenced literature

Skills

1. Critical reading

2. Group work and processing

3. Writing analysis

4. Publishing a newspaper

5. Oral presentation

6. Interviewing and note taking

7. Recognizing and using literary devices

8. Writing from different points of view

9. Creating organizers and charts

10. Following time constraints

Concepts

1. Relating folktales to society
2. Reading autobiography as literature
3. Understanding the relationship of Romanticism to American literature
4. Understanding allusion in literature activates/expands reader's knowledge
5. Relating American literature to American society
6. Working with oratory as a literary form

Assessment

1. Teacher assessment of mutually agreed-on student goals
2. Teacher and student assessment of individual and group work
3. Peer evaluation of effort and input into project work
4. Teachers' shared assessment of cooperative activities between classes
5. Teacher evaluation of written student work (Highlights of the English portion of this unit are presented in Figure 4–1)

FIGURE 4–1   English Highlights: A New World—A New Literature

Focus Points	Facts	Skills	Concepts
1. Revolution	1. Folktales and legends	1. Critical reading	1. Relationship of folktales to a society
2. Forming a new government	2. Authors: Irving, Bryant, and Cooper	2. Analytic writing	2. Relationship of American Romanticism to American literature
3. Birth of American literature	3. Characteristics of Romanticism	3. Group processing	3. Literature as a reflection of society

Sample Activities:

1. Students will complete an advance organizer activity answering: "What is an American?" This will engage students as well as develop a cultural touchstone for the unit.

2. Students will read and analyze the writings of Ben Franklin. Especially noting contributions, insights, and reflections about Colonial society and its influences.

3. Students will read a historical fiction novel concentrating on setting, daily life, historic characteristics and characters, and key themes.

THE SOCIAL STUDIES FOCUS

Materials

1. American Studies text
2. Supplementary readings provided by the teacher

114

3. Student-generated organizers, maps, and other materials

4. Videos

5. Library resource materials

Activities and Time

1. During the first week of the unit, the emphasis is on the French and Indian War. Students begin the study of this era by drawing a map of the colonies at the time of the French and Indian War. Through textual reading, students locate and create organizers graphically depicting the causes of this war and its effects on the economy and people of the colonies. In completing this portion of the unit, students examine the effect of the events in Europe on the colonies.

2. During the second week, the class creates a chart of the various attempts by the English to recoup their losses from the war and the specific taxes and acts that were put into effect. The American Studies students read three excerpts from Crevecoeur, Thomas Paine, and Patrick Henry as homework in preparation for the discussion. Following the discussion, students also write a two- to three-page paper exploring the theme of "What it means to be an American" from the point of view of a prerevolutionary American colonist. Essays are shared and assessed by both teachers.

3. During the third week, students will continue to examine the effects of English actions on the American colonists. Cause-and-effect organizers delineating each British action are constructed and presented. Students also examine the events in Lexington, Concord, and Boston for their impact on the colonies. As a preparation for the joint class activity, students write a one-page reaction, from a colonist's point of view, to the events in Boston and what they personally feel about recent events. The classes are then brought together to discuss, to prepare, and to debate signing the Declaration of Independence. Two to three days should be set aside for this joint activity.

4. Weeks 4 and 5 are devoted to a study of the American Revolution. Students design an annotated timeline showing the progression of events from the beginning of the French and Indian War through the signing of the Declaration of Independence. This timeline should be updated as the study of the war continues. Students should also update the map that was drawn earlier in the unit to show the status of the colonies at the time of the revolution. Students update the status of the map by noting locations of important battles and events. To study the war, students should create charts showing the major battles, the leaders, and the importance and effects of their actions. Charts should be completed for the war in the north, in the south, and at sea. Students follow up with activities on the reasons, causes, and effects of the American victory.

   This portion of the unit concludes with a "Who Am I?" (for a more detailed description of the activity, see Nowicki & Meehan, 1996) on major figures of the unit such as George Washington, Thomas Jefferson, Crispus Attucks, and a variety of others. Allow one day of class time for library research and two days for the presentation. Assessment is based on thoroughness of research, seriousness and depth of presentation, characterization, and costuming.

5. Weeks 6 and 7 consist of readings and activities exploring postwar problems, the movement west, and early Indian policies, map work on the changing face of the New World, Shay's Rebellion, the Articles of Confederation, the role of women and blacks in the new country, and the growing need for a change in the form of government. Students should look closely at the new spirit of Republicanism that was prevalent in the country. Possible activities include placing Daniel Shay on trial for treason, student designed new towns for the Northwest Territory, a thought question (again for a detailed description of this activity see Nowicki and Meehan, 1996) probing people's reasons for becoming pioneers, and various organizers showing cause-and-effect changes in the new country.

6. A constitutional convention with the classes operating together highlights the eighth week of the unit. Members of the history class role-play various historical persona representing key ideas and attitudes of those delegates attending the convention. Debate on major issues, from slavery to states' rights, can be reenacted for students to gain an understanding of the compromise and struggle to create the law of the land.

7. The final week of the unit is for examining the Constitution of the United States and the Bill of Rights. Working in groups, students create charts to represent visually the separation of powers, the credentials for office and the process by which a bill becomes a law. Each group presents the material and teaches that part of the Constitution to the class. Case studies highlight key portions and the rights contained in the Bill of Rights. Of special interest are those areas that deal with student freedoms. As a final project, students invite a lawyer to discuss the case studies and students' interpretations. Student assessment of this area of the unit includes a take-home test on the Constitution emphasizing the importance of the document and the rights it affords us.

Factual Material

The list of factual material for a unit of this scope is a long one and includes people, places, events, decisions, causes and effects, and dates, as well as other material brought out in the course of research and presentation

Skills

1. Creating timelines

2. Creating organizers, charts, and graphs to depict information

3. Oral presentation skills

4. Integrating research into historical personae

5. Learning to budget time

6. Developing cooperative and collaborative work skills

7. Utilizing each other as resources

8. Writing analytically about history

9. Working with cause-and-effect relationships

Concepts

1. Government as a means of controlling society

2. War as a means to achieving nationalistic goals

3. The relationship of compromise to argument

4. Conflict as a stimulant to progress

5. The relationship of individual actions to societal change

6. Democracy as a form of government

7. How unresolved problems of the past create problems in the future

8. The influence of geographic location on economic function

Assessment

1. Teacher assessment of mutually established goals

2. Student and teacher assessment of oral and written work

3. Student self-assessment

4. Peer evaluation of effort and attitude in group work

5. Assessment of affective goals by student and teacher

6. Cooperative teacher assessment of goal mastery (highlights of the social studies portion of this unit are presented in Figure 4–2)

FIGURE 4–2 Social Studies Highlights: A New World—A New Literature

Focus Points	Facts	Skills	Concepts
1. American Revolution	1. Major dates	1. Creating timelines	1. Government as control
2. Formation of a democratic republic	2. Colonial and British leaders	2. Oral presentations	2. Democracy as a form of government
3. The growth of a country	3. Tax acts	3. Integrating research into a presentation	3. Influence of geography on economic functions

Sample Activities:

1. Students will complete a series of organizers depicting causes, conduct, and effects of the French and Indian War.

2. Students will read and analyze writing of Crevecoeur, Paine, and Henry to gain insights into the mood and character of the country. After discussion, students will write a short paper, from the point of view of an American colonist about "What it means to be an American."

3. Through readings, discussions, charts, maps, and graphic organizers, students will study the revolution. Part of this will include a "Who am I?" exercise.

COMMON LINKAGES

Materials

1. Respective texts in each class

2. Student notes, organizers, and maps

3. Additional supplementary material from library sources

4. Teacher-prepared supplementary readings and materials

ACTIVITIES AND TIME

1. During week 2 of the unit, the two classes are brought together, and the English students share with the history students the themes and beliefs of Crevecoeur, Patrick Henry, and Thomas Paine. History students share the temper of the times, which initiated such fervent beliefs. Students then write a two- to three-page essay explaining "What it means to be an American" from the point of view of a colonist of the times. Essays are shared with the classes and assessed cooperatively by the teachers. Approximately two days should be allowed for this unit.

2. The Declaration of Independence is another shared document studied during week 3. Students in the English class analyze the stylistic devices that charge the theme with its power. History students share interpretation of the document through a cause-and-effect relationship. Students then assume historical personae and prepare a debate on the question of whether to sign the Declaration of Independence. Concluding the debate, students submit an essay explaining their reasons. (Approximately 2–3 days)

3. The next scheduled joint meeting is in week 6 of the unit. During the period from the end of the Revolution to the ratification of the Constitution, a number of changes affected the new country. The growing spirit of republicanism was reflected in the writings of Washington Irving, William Cullen Bryant, and James Fenimore Cooper. As the English students are completing their study of the authors, the classes are brought together to share the themes of the writers and the prevailing attitudes of the country. Following the common activities, students write an essay on how the spirit of republicanism is obvious in one of the works of the three writers. (Approximately 2–3 days)

4. The Constitutional Convention is a highlight of the cooperative class study. During week 8 of the unit, the history class prepares and presents the Constitutional Convention, which is chronicled by the English class, who publish a newspaper detailing the week's events, actions, and people and serving as a permanent record of the activity and a source for review. (Approximately 5 days)

5. The final joint activity is a discussion with a lawyer of the key rights guaranteed in the Bill of Rights. Students write a reaction paper detailing how one of the cases influenced their thinking. (1 day)

Total Shared Time: Approximately 11–14 days

Skills

1. Developing cooperative and collaborative work skills
2. Developing positive social skills
3. Researching supplementary material
4. Integrating supplementary material into oral and written presentations
5. Integrating historical data into fictional pieces
6. Organizing materials and locations
7. Reading and writing critically
8. Creating links between social science and language arts
9. Recognizing the difference between fact and myth

Concepts

1. The relationship of literary themes to historical attitudes
2. The relationship of history to present beliefs and values
3. Government as a system for creating an orderly society
4. Argument as a tool for determining the soundness of ideas
5. Literature as a record of humans' struggle for truth
6. How the ideas of human beings influencing the course of history
7. How the course of history influences the ideas of humans (highlights are noted in Figure 4–3)

FIGURE 4–3 Interdisciplinary Activities: A New World—A New Literature

Interdisciplinary Objectives	Shared Skills	Shared Concepts
1. Working with cause-and-effect relationships	1. Researching supplementary material	1. Relationship of literary themes and historical attitudes
2. Developing greater understanding of American culture	2. Integrating historical material into fictional pieces	2. Literature as a record of the human search for truth
3. Recognizing the importance of chronology in growing process	3. Creating links between social sciences and language arts	3. How the course of history influences the ideas of people

Sample Activities:

1. Students will share insights into the meaning and style of writing inherent in the Declaration of Independence. This will conclude with a debate over the reasons for signing the document.

2. Students will conduct a constitutional convention, which will be documented through a student-designed and student-published newspaper.

3. Students will participate in a discussion of the Bill of Rights with an attorney.

SUMMARY

Combining the study of American history and American literature is certainly exciting, stimulating, and comprehensive. It allows students to recognize that, at times, connections between the two disciplines are very tight, sometimes to the point that it is hard to separate the specific subject areas. The Declaration of Independence provides such an example. To appreciate fully the power and intensity of its ideas, students must decode the stylistic devices and powerful syntax of the document. To understand fully the impact of such a document, however, it must be studied in the context of the times that nurtured its creation. The lines between literature and social science are blurred and may even disappear. For students, a linked unit emphasizing the importance of political ideas and literary themes leaves them with a heightened awareness of the tenor of the times and of the importance of literature as a reflection of human needs and feelings.

Although English and social studies run parallel on a chronological framework, many common themes exist that teachers can emphasize and coordinate. Themes such as individualism, a quest, the nature of human beings, the American dream/nightmare, transformations, immigration and the immigrant experience, the search for justice, courage, and nature and freedom are readily adaptable to both disciplines. Teachers need look no further than the fiery oratory of Patrick Henry and his "treasonous" remarks to understand the themes of courage, justice, and the fight for ideals. Studying the writings of James Fenimore Cooper elicits parallels with individuals who journeyed to find freedom and personal fulfillment and, in the process, displayed courage. The list could go on; these few models are offered as guides and inspirations to teachers.

A note about references: Most of the material needed for the development of this unit is available within respective departments. Each unit can be taught and paralleled easily through the use of basic anthologies; however, the search for materials need not stop there. Many resources exist to supplement such a study. *Cobblestone Magazine,* published by Cobblestone Press of Peterborough, New Hampshire, is an excellent source, which, though directed to social studies classes, is equally valuable to language arts teachers. For more in-depth examples of conventions, debates, and mock trials, Nowicki and Meehan's *The Collaborative Social Studies Classroom* offers a number of models easily adapted to secondary classrooms. We have found that including the librarian in the initial discussions of unit building is not only helpful, but absolutely necessary. The librarian's knowledge of existing sources and access to other supplements can save teachers time and prevent student frustration when adequate material cannot be located.

Finally, for the purpose of defining a unit, we offer suggested time frames for the activities. This is not a hard and fast schedule but only a framework of the amount of time we have needed to complete various units. Additionally, when two classes, teachers, and interdisciplinary activities are involved, it is imperative that both teachers have a keen idea of scope and sequence. Managing time is important, but the real key to an interdisciplinary unit is to involve students in recognizing that learning is broad and comprehensive, not compartmental and restricted.

UNIT-LENGTH THEMES

Title: World War I: Countries—Battles—People

Subject Areas: English and Social Studies

Ages/Grades: Grade 9

Number of Students: Full class of 40–45 students

Focus Points:
1. Social, economic and political conditions in Europe in the late 1800s and early 1900s
2. Causes of World War I
3. Impact of war on society
4. World War I as a cause of World War II

Time Necessary: Approximately 8–10 weeks

OVERVIEW

By the time the study of World Wars I and II arrives in the school year, students have worked extensively to gain an understanding of history and reason for studying past civilizations and cultures, and have encountered many ideas about the nature of society and humans. When we enter this time period, ninth graders begin to see true connections. They have seen movies about the wars and may have encountered some of the literature. They see that they have finally reached a century numbered with the same first two digits as their own. Consequently, they can now begin to focus on direct links from the actions and events of a time period to their own world and society. Although they have worked at comparisons all year, linkages are not always obvious. Even though we create elaborate plans to compare Greek and Roman civilization to government structures, literary forms, entertainment, and architecture, ninth graders still see these ideas as far removed. With the world wars, there are direct lines drawn from a period of time that they can comprehend. From grandparents and great-grandparents, they may still hear the stories of these eras. Many have grandparents who fought in World War II and have seen the veterans parade on holidays.

Additionally, this is a time period that, as ninth graders need to see, effected great change in the political structure of the world. Today's students are familiar with the term *global community* from the various news media. They need to see that World War I had a direct impact on creating a knowledge of the world's influence through developments in war, communications, and transportation.

Recording these events were the writers, poets, playwrights, sculptors, painters, and others who sought to understand society and individuals' behavior in a world that found itself in total war. At this point, ninth graders need to work with larger connections. Teachers must go further than making historical linkages from the past to the present. They need to look at interdisciplinary connections that will meet, reinforce, and go beyond one subject area. For teachers truly to involve students in their learning, as we have stated many times, students must see the connections between disciplines.

To highlight one connection briefly, look at the options available from a skill-based activity of creating a map of World War I Europe. Although this appears subject-specific to social studies, it has implications for language arts as well. While serving a geographic base for social studies, it can also become a record of the literature. Ninth graders can locate Flanders Field from reading the poem of that name, the railway station in Pirandello's *War*, and the battlefield for "And the Band Played Waltzing Matilda." Suddenly, for these students, the activity becomes an integral part of a portfolio connecting the two courses. The end result is the reinforcement of skills, places, and events through their efforts in two classes rather than the limited perspective of one course.

This model lists the facts, skills, and concepts from each discipline. It includes the objectives and goals of each teacher as they create a scope and sequence for the unit. Additionally, this model offers a listing of activities that foster affective skills as students work cooperatively and collaboratively in completing the assignments. All activities have been designed and tested using students in heterogeneously grouped ninth-grade classrooms. These activities are not meant to be an inflexible structure but are merely a guideline, a series of suggestions that may be expanded and modified on the basis of the needs of different classrooms and teacher expectations. Finally, the activities allow students to be the creators of their knowledge as they work with the facts, polish their skills, and build conceptual frameworks that allow them to understand their culture better.

INTERDISCIPLINARY OBJECTIVES:

1. Students will develop an understanding of the connections between literature and social studies.

2. Students will work with cause-and-effect relationships.

3. Students will work with gathering and interpreting information from a variety of sources.

4. Student will learn to participate in cooperative work experiences.

5. Students will work at manipulating facts and skills to create personal conceptual frameworks.

6. Students will develop frameworks for presenting and sharing information.

INTRODUCTION

In this unit, which lasts an average of eight to ten weeks, a ninth-grade social studies class and a ninth-grade English class will examine the social, political, and economic impact of political alliances and world war. Particular focus will be on the cause-and-effect relationships of countries, the struggle of individuals dealing with conflict, and the connections between the two disciplines.

A central point in the unit is the ability of the English and social studies teachers to define the type of teaching to use at various times within the unit. Certain time is required for subject-specific material; other time is needed for teaming and parallel teaching; still other time may be used for bringing the groups together for common activities.

THE ENGLISH CLASS FOCUS

Materials

1. Short story anthologies

2. Poetry anthologies

3. Additional teacher-supplied readings

4. Core novel

5. Student journals

Activities and Time

1. Students read four short stories that depict themes related to conflict, survival, societal change, the American dream/nightmare, and individual struggle as seen during the time period. Students keep a reaction journal to each story, create a theme chart comparing themes, write a short analytic paper on a jointly determined aspect of literary device, create a plot analysis organizer for each story, and write a short story exploring one of the themes from the stories. (3 weeks)

2. Students read a novel based on events, actions, or themes of the time period 1890–1940. Each student keeps a journal as she or he reads the novel. The novel selected may vary as long it is from the era.) In addition to the journal, students select activities from the following list to complete as they read or after finishing. (2 weeks)

   a. Make a character chart.   b. Make a plot organizer.

   c. Design a book jacket.   d. Make a theme analysis paper.

   e. Write another chapter.   f. Script a scene.

   g. Analyze a character.   h. Write an author letter.

3. Students read eight to ten poems and/or songs dealing with themes of the era. For each selection, they write a reaction paper, analyzing style and content. Students write a poem or song of their own continuing one of the themes. (1 week)

4. Students experiment with various forms of writing based on class activities, videos, or discussions. Students are required to complete each of the following: a letter home from the front or to the front, a newspaper report of an action at home or at the front, an essay responding to a key idea about the meaning of war and the reasons for war. (2 weeks)

Total Time: 8 weeks

Factual Material

Facts as determined by the selections of readings and writers; elements of literature such as characterization, plot, setting, theme, denouement, conflict, and climax; genres of literature such as poem, short story, novel, or play; writing devices such as alliteration, symbol, irony, metaphor, point of view, hyperbole, and personification

Skills

1. Critical reading and thinking

2. Cooperative and collaborative work skills

3. Writing skills—fiction, nonfiction, poetry

4. Group or individual presentation

5. Manipulation of facts and concepts through organizers

6. Maintaining a journal

Concepts

1. Use of literature experience

2. Literature as a means of seeking truth

3. Literature as a product of its time

4. Conflict as a foundation of literature

5. Writing as a record of human activity

6. Role of the individual within society

Assessment

1. Student self-evaluation based on goals

2. Peer evaluation or reaction

3. Teacher evaluation of student-written work

4. Teacher evaluation of group presentation

5. Teacher or student evaluation of affective behaviors (English highlights are presented in Figure 4–4)

FIGURE 4–4   English Highlights: World War I: Countries—Battles—People

Focus Points	Facts	Skills	Concepts
1. Social conditions in Europe and in the late 1800s and early 1900s	1. Literary terms	1. Critical reading	1. Literature as a product of its times
2. Causes of World War I	2. Genres of literature	2. Maintaining a journal	2. Conflict as a foundation of literature
3. Impact of war on society	3. Key writers of the period	3. Creating organizers	3. Role of the individual within society

FIGURE 4–4 *(continued)*

Sample Activities:

1. Students will read, journal, and create theme charts of various short stories depicting themes of conflict, survival, and societal change.

2. Students will read a historical novel relevant to the era and complete an activity on a cultural and literary aspect of the novel.

3. Students will study songs and poetry of the era, especially noting theme, style, and content. Students will create a personal piece imitating style and theme.

THE SOCIAL STUDIES CLASS FOCUS

Materials

1. World History text

2. Atlas

3. Supplementary readings

4. Student-created maps and charts

5. Teacher-prepared supplementary readings

Activities and Time

1. Students create a series of three maps of Europe, in the late 1800s, during World War I, and after the war, showing the realignment of boundaries. (1 week)

2. Students are responsible for locating, defining, and identifying a list of approximately fifty people, places, events, decisions, alliances, and governments of the era. (1 week)

3. Students prepare a television news show documenting the events at Sarajevo and the assassination of the archduke. Students will be assigned to groups to prepare segments on the people involved, the background to the crime, the conditions in Europe, the events of the day, and the obvious effects of the event on the world. (1 week)

4. Working in groups of 3 to 4, students create and present graphic organizers demonstrating causes, alliances, people, chain of events, battles, weapons, and effects of World War I. (1 week)

5. Students view the film *All Quiet on the Western Front.* They keep a journal as they view it and, at the end, write a paper dealing with theme and content. (1 week)

6. Each student, in costume, presents a four- to six-minute "Who Am I?" of an important person of the era. The person need not be a military or political leader but should be someone who represents a viewpoint of the era. Students submit a written paper about their character and have an activity for the class based on the "Who Am I?" (1 week)

7. Students reconstruct the Paris peace talks following the armistice. Students role-play historical characters and points of view. They conduct

library research to help support their views. They prepare written scripts to use in the videotaped reconstruction. (1 week)

8. Students examine the postwar period and the social, political, and economic conditions that the war created. Students explore such things as the influenza epidemic, the realignment of boundaries, nationalism, militarism, imperialism, worldwide economic depression, and political upheaval as a way of exploring the causes of World War II. Significant time will be spent in reading and reacting to the ideas through short papers and thought questions. Students will write a short paper on how World War I lead to World War II. (1 week)

Total Time: 8 weeks

Factual Material

People, places, events, actions, decisions, alliances, and so on that are common to the World War I era; statistics of the era on casualties, population, and so on; map details

Skills

1. Creating timelines
2. Cartography
3. Creating graphic organizers to explain material
4. Reading charts
5. Create historical personae
6. Separating fact from opinion

Concepts

1. Understanding the role of chance in altering history
2. Seeing the excesses of nationalism as a cause for war
3. Understanding the desire for territory and resources as a cause of conflict
4. Understanding war as a means to dominate and conquer
5. Seeing how injustices create anger and hatred that fuel a desire for revenge

Assessment

1. Student self-evaluation based on goals
2. Peer evaluation of group work and presentations
3. Teacher evaluation of oral and written work
4. Teacher evaluation of final test
5. Student mastery of specified facts and skills (social studies highlights are presented in Figure 4–5)

FIGURE 4–5   Social Studies Highlights: World War I: Countries—Battles—People

Focus Points	Facts	Skills	Concepts
1. Political conditions in Europe in the late 1800s and early 1900s	1. People, places, and events	1. Cartography	1. Historical change
2. Causes of war	2. World War I	2. Creating annotated timelines	2. Excesses of nationalism
3. World War I as a direct cause of World War II	3. Alliances and specifics of the peace conference	3. Reading charts	3. How injustices fuel the desire for revenge

Sample Activities:

1. Students will create a series of maps showing changes that occurred in European boundaries.

2. Students will prepare a news documentary show delineating causes and effects of the assassination of the archduke of Austria-Hungary.

3. Students will assume historical roles and reenact the Paris Peace Talks.

COMMON LINKAGES

Materials

1. Student-generated work (writings, charts, organizers)

2. Texts used in each class

3. Supplementary readings

4. Videotapes of any presentations

Activities and Time

1. Working in groups of four, two from each class, students use the social studies–generated maps and note locations from literature such as birthplaces and locations of events and journeys. (1 day)

2. The two classes are brought together to create a newsmagazine similar in format to a *Newsweek* year-end review issue. Groups are composed of a mixture of students from each class (two from each is a good blend). Students are assigned areas to complete such as entertainment, books, politics, lead stories, world sections, art, milestones, sports, and news of the year in review. This issue also contains artwork, pictures, advertisements, opinion or editorial pieces (including political cartoons), and a cover suitable to the issue's content. The end product is copied and distributed to each student, and becomes a powerful artifact of the classes' joint efforts. (1–2 weeks)

3. All students keep a journal throughout that addresses issue common to the unit. The final part of the journal is an "I learned that . . ." stressing the overall learnings that have occurred in the process. (Continuous)

4. Pair or group students, with one and one or two and two from each group to create a timeline of the era noting events from a historical perspective and from the perspective of literature and the arts. Depending on the time constraints, this can be a simple one-day activity with concise notations and dates, or it can be spread out over three days and can add illustrations and graphics to the timeline to make it more interesting. (1 day; 2–3 days)

Skills

1. Working collaboratively to share information
2. Organizing and writing a journal
3. Using notes and graphs
4. Writing, editing, proofreading
5. Publishing
6. Developing timelines
7. Creating and using maps
8. Depicting ideas in concrete drawings

Concepts

1. Help literature and history are interrelated
2. Increases one's understanding of historical perspective by understanding people
3. Cause-and-effect relationships as seen in the context of their time
4. Learning from the past by studying its history and its culture

Assessment

1. Teacher commentary on the journals
2. Self-evaluation of student-generated materials
3. Student and teacher evaluation of the final magazine
4. Student and teacher assessment of affective behaviors in collaborative efforts (interdisciplinary highlights are presented in Figure 4–6)

SUMMARY

This unit offers ninth-grade students and teachers the opportunity to work together in a nonthreatening, mutually rewarding teaching/learning experience. It shares a time period when the world was undergoing a radical change and approaches the events, people, places, and ideas from two different perspectives, then brings them together to show the common links.

The unit builds throughout the term as students' skill levels increase and dual reinforcement increases confidence. Consequently, the final common

FIGURE 4–6 Interdisciplinary Activities: World War I: Countries—Battles—People

Interdisciplinary Objectives	Shared Skills	Shared Concepts
1. Making connections between literature and social studies	1. Using notes and graphics in presentations	1. How literature and history are intertwined
2. Participating in group activities	2. Publishing	2. How understanding people increases one's understanding of historical perspective
3. Creating personal conceptual frameworks	3. Creating and using maps	3. How people learn of the past by studying its history and culture

Sample Activities:

1. Working together, classes will create a news magazine with specific sections, such as world, nation, arts, entertainment, sports, and milestones, to capture the flavor of an era.

2. Students will use maps produced in social studies class to note locations from fictional readings.

3. Students will create annotated timelines showing key dates in history, the arts, and literature.

projects are not intimidating mountains to cross but, rather, a companionable sharing of the view from the heightened perspective at the top. By sharing the knowledge from both English and social studies, students arrive at a broader knowledge base, which generalizes their learning and becomes synthesized into their realm. Future connections will be easier with this common foundation on which to build.

Important for teachers to note is that each teacher maintains the integrity of his or her discipline as they address subject-specific learnings. However, they gradually work to the next higher step of learning as they parallel each other through the basic themes and the commonality of the era and content of the war. The unit is open enough for teachers to experiment and come together at a number of places. The nature of the activity-centered instruction lends itself to pairing activities through content, theme, or skills.

A number of themes can be brought into the unit and examined from both perspectives: survival, humans' inhumanity to humans, pride, greed, abuse and corruption of power, creativity, manipulation, values, morals, ideals, sacrifice, alienation, isolation, and a myriad of others that offer another hook to bring the two areas together. The possibilities are limited only by the creativity, enthusiasm, and ambition of the two teachers involved.

A NOTE ABOUT RESOURCE MATERIAL

We have intentionally left the specific texts and supplementary readings up to the teachers who will design their own units. Availability of materials varies widely from school to school. Additionally, for the unit to succeed, it is best for teachers to use material with which they are familiar and which they believe is best for their students. There are countless short stories about war in general and World War I in particular. English anthologies generally have an abundant supply of poetry by the trench poets of World War I, and the music is available in many public libraries if not in the school itself. Kerry Meehan

129

particularly recommends songs such as Pete St. John's "When Margaret Was Eleven" and "The Town I Loved So Well." Other folk music selections are "And the Band Played Waltzing Matilda" and "The Green Fields of France." We mention these because, though not widely known, they create powerful reactions in the students.

Some Hints and Notes

This unit provides opportunities for parallel teaching, teaming, and team teaching. Although schedules work against this type of teaching activity, this should not stop motivated teachers from trying the unit. The teachers involved should stay in close contact with each other concerning the skills, themes, and concepts that they are teaching at the time. When students know that teachers are sharing ideas in these areas, there is a positive effect on student involvement.

Another way to work out the last unit of preparing a magazine is for the teachers to schedule an in-school field trip and use it to bring the two classes together for a full activity day. Effectively organized, with students having preset information about group members, assignment, and expectations, a great deal can be accomplished in this time frame. We have both met with success in a similar format by holding Greek Olympics and cultural studies comparisons. The secret is not to let school logistics defeat you. The rewards will truly surpass the limitations that must be navigated.

To close this section, look again at the nature of the classes involved. Both classes rely on activity-centered, cooperatively working students, sharing knowledge and information to reach a greater concept. Our experience clearly demonstrates that for heterogeneous and interdisciplinary education to work, it must be activity-centered and cooperative. Turning students free to interact, share, argue, struggle, and arrive at a final product through trial and error is itself the greatest interdisciplinary model we can offer.

UNIT-LENGTH THEMES

Title:	The Medieval World—Anything But the Dark Ages
Subject Areas:	English and Social Studies
Ages/Grades:	Grade 9
Number of Students:	Full class of 40–45 students
Focus Points:	1. The power of the church
	2. Organizational structures
	3. Cultural developments
	4. Growth of towns, cities, and nations
	5. Historical events
	6. Inventions
Time Necessary:	Approximately 8–10 weeks

OVERVIEW

The Middle Ages is a historic time period that offers a wealth of possibilities for creating an interdisciplinary unit. Many students already have some ideas about knights, Robin Hood, and King Arthur. Even if they are not familiar with the people and themes, the very nature of the Middle Ages lends itself to high activity, student-centered learning.

Generally, at this point in the year, ninth graders have completed units on prehistory, early humans, Egypt, Greece, and Rome. They are beginning to develop a personal sense of history, to see patterns developing in the growth of civilization and culture, and to understand a chronology in history that progresses through cause-and-effect relationships. Additionally, they have been developing skills and making maps, timelines, organizers, and charts to interpret text and support ideas. Similarly, students in language arts classes have further developed their writing skills and are more proficient at recognizing and writing about theme, as well as gaining insight into the nature, genres, and development of literature.

If teachers have not made connections between the two disciplines, the medieval era is an area to consider. It also makes sense educationally. The Middle Ages can easily lend itself to a unit steeped in factual knowledge. There are so many people, places, events, and documents that coverage becomes an issue solved by a quick reading and objective test. However as Greenlaw and colleagues tell us, "If one is to get beyond the surface facts of history to the underlying structure and meaning, it will take more than a cursory reading of a textbook" (Greenlaw, Shepperson, & Nistler, 1992, p. 200). As we have stressed many times, facts are the starting point, but true learning that creates imprinting and develops within the learner the ability to generalize that knowledge to other areas must have a broader scope. Again, Shepperson et al. support our contention, "that literature must be an integral part of the [social studies] curriculum" (1992, p. 200).

Like our other units, this one is created to offer flexible guidelines and suggestions for putting the unit together. It is critical, however, for teachers to have the time to determine which skills and facts are subject-specific and which should be developed mutually. As part of their planning time, teachers must decide whether they want to teach by paralleling, teaming, or team teaching. Unfortunately, some latitude in choosing the format may be limited by a schedule into which teachers are locked. With the knowledge of their unique logistical problems, however, teachers can still create options. This unit can be structured easily to any of the three formats.

This unit is best appreciated by fully bringing the Middle Ages alive through the experience of students planning a medieval fair day. This activity serves as a culminating event but, more important, serves as a foundation on which to structure and build many of the unit activities. Teachers must create a schedule that will allow sufficient time for planning and preparing for the fair.

Additionally, it is important for teachers planning this unit to identify topics and events in each area that will allow for interdisciplinary activity. One example might be in the study of the Magna Carta. While the social studies class might examine this document in terms of its cause-and-effect impact on medieval society, the students in the language arts class might create poems or songs to be presented by bards and minstrels celebrating the concept of freedom. While the social studies class is examining the structure of the manor or the monastery, the English students could be writing a short story set on a manor, working on a characterization of a monk, or preparing a newspaper published by the monastery or manor. These activities are as numerous as the involved teachers can create.

This model delineates the facts, skills, and concepts for each discipline. It includes objectives and goals for each teacher as well as a list of interdisciplinary concepts. Additionally, this model offers a variety of activities that foster and nurture collaborative work. Models support our philosophy that learning must be active, cooperative, heterogeneous, and involving. The concern is not with coverage but with stimulating student involvement that develops the ability to solve problems, think critically, and put to use the knowledge that they are developing. Additionally, the activities follow the model of first developing a vocabulary of facts to hone skills so they might create larger constructs representing their learning. Some of the activities are also created for students to have fun. Fun raises morale, which leads to a more harmonious and pleasant workplace for all.

INTERDISCIPLINARY OBJECTIVES

1. Students will develop an understanding of the connections between literature and social studies.

2. Students will work with cause-and-effect relationships.

3. Students will work with gathering and interpreting information from a variety of sources.

4. Students will develop cooperative work skills.

5. Students will work at manipulating facts and skills to create personal conceptual frameworks.

6. Students will develop frameworks for presenting and sharing information.

7. Students will develop the skills to differentiate between fact and fiction, myth and reality.

8. Students will develop the organizational skills necessary to produce comprehensive and collaborative culminating activities.

INTRODUCTION

In this unit, which will last approximately 8 to 10 weeks, one academic term, ninth-grade social studies and English classes will examine the political, social, economic, cultural, and religious influences that define the Middle Ages as a period of history and of literature. Of particular importance in this unit are the connections between the two disciplines as students come to understand how literature reflects the society that creates history.

This unit is created primarily for teachers who wish to parallel-teach. It first establishes the subject-specific skills and facts that form the foundation for the activities. It next involves teaming as the classes create a medieval festival to celebrate their learning about a way of life. As the unit unfolds, teachers must have a firm idea of the breadth and scope of the fair; where it will be; and what activities, events, foods, entertainments, and costumes will be included in it. Teachers need to keep in mind the amount of class time throughout the unit that needs to be set aside for planning and preparing the festival. Our experience has taught us to allow one to two days throughout the first six to seven weeks, with a block of five or six days at the end for polishing and logistics. Should the festival be too broad for teachers who are just beginning to experiment with interdisciplinary work, the activity can be downsized to a banquet. (See the shorter activities in Chapter 3 for details on this structure.)

THE ENGLISH CLASS FOCUS

Materials

1. Assorted novels set in the Middle Ages

2. Selected poetry and songs

3. A basic anthology with a medieval component

4. Teacher-prepared supplementary readings/activities

5. Student-prepared materials, graphs, charts, and notes

6. Videos

Activities and Time

1. Week 1 is spent in completing an advance organizer (for a description of one style of advance organizer, see Joyce & Weil, 1972) to determine what students know and to stimulate previous learning.

   a. Place students into groups of three or four to brainstorm, categorize, and classify the abstract qualities of a Hero. Students create a graphic organizer to explain their idea to the class. Following class discussion, each student writes a one-page definition of a hero.

b. The second phase of the organizer is a concept attainment exercise whereby students determine the definitions of a legend, a folktale, and a myth by analyzing and comparing examples of each type.

c. After working through these first two exercises, students quickly research these genres of literature and compare the definitions they find to their own. Students share research and polish their own definitions.

d. Students now write a short story fitting the definition that each has created and edited. The first draft of the story should be due on the second Monday of the unit. Students polish and rewrite the story according to process-writing guidelines established within the class. Final due dates vary and are mutually agreed on by student and teacher.

2. During the second and third weeks, students read myths of King Arthur and the Knights of the Round Table. They create charts and organizers comparing the characters to the definition of the Hero. Elements of the medieval romance are introduced through a concept attainment exercise as students relate their definitions to the exploits in the readings. During the course of the reading period, students work on characterization, elements of setting, daily life in the Middle Ages, themes, and influences on the characters. Students complete organizers and write reaction pieces to specific skill and content areas. Also during the second week, students select an appropriate novel dealing with the medieval period for reading on their own, outside of class. The novel must be completed by Friday of the fifth week of the unit. As they read, students complete a journal noting characteristics of the Hero myth and folktales, medieval characteristics, daily life and activities, and their personal reactions. As students share journals with the teacher, a mutually agreed-on final paper or project on the work is decided.

Additionally, students complete their individual choice of a personally created book jacket for the novel or an advertisement for the novel that will be featured during the medieval fair.

3. Week 4 is a poetry and song week. This can be done during class time to give students more time to work on independent reading and short stories if needed. In addition to specific activities geared to figures of speech, metaphor, personification, rhyme, and meter, students read a variety of medieval poetry and songs. A short paper is completed for Friday of that week on life, love, emotions, and thoughts in the Middle Ages as depicted in these works. Additionally, each student is responsible for writing an original piece of poetry for the beginning of week 5 that imitates the theme and style, rhyme, and meter of the pieces studied.

4. Week 5 begins with a sharing of the poems and songs created by the students. Ideally, the next step can be worked out with the art teacher, but if that is not possible there are many picture books and other sources

to use for help. Students create an "illustrated manuscript" of their poems in the style of Celtic script used by monks. Samples from the *Book of Kells* are helpful to show students the intricacy of the work. This activity takes a few days. The student-selected novel is due on Friday of this week.

5. Week 6 is dedicated to working with the independent novel that the students have read. There are a variety of ways to work through this activity. The following list is not comprehensive but merely gives some examples of the types of activities that work well in a heterogeneous classroom. Obviously, teachers know which activity would work best with certain students.

   a. Group together students who read the same work for discussion activities.

   b. Students may draw a map of the book tracing the hero's journey.

   c. Students can identify the protagonist and the antagonist and draw a comparison/contrast organizer (to be described) to examine the two. This can provide the basis for an essay.

   d. Artistically talented students might illustrate two or three scenes that are important to the theme of the book.

   e. Students can draw a storyboard for a movie treatment of the work.

   f. Students can write a letter to the author dealing with questions or problems that they might want the author to clarify.

   g. Students can choose two significant passages and explain in essay form why these are important to the development of theme in the novel.

   h. Students can write a newspaper account of an event in the novel or a newspaper obituary of one of the characters.

   i. Students can interview a character in the novel. They can be creative with this by pairing off and, in costume, role playing the interview on videotape.

6. Week 7 is the week for presentations on the novels and establishing roles and duties for the festival.

7. Week 8 is filled with specific preparations for the festival, which ideally will be held on Friday of that week to bring a neat closure to the unit.

8. All students maintain journals throughout the activity. Teachers should give them time at least three days a week to write in their journals about the activities in which they are involved, what they learned, and what they think of them. These journals form the basis of a final two- to three-page paper on what the activity meant to students and what they learned during the course of the unit. Students should grade themselves individually for the unit at the end of this writing.

Total Time: 8 weeks

Factual Material

Literary terms that come up in the discussions and readings: myth, folktale, hero, quest, romance, lay, minstrel, troubadour, bard, and so on; poetry terms: rhyme, meter, scansion, symbol, metaphor, simile, synecdoche, and others; people, places, and terms that are included in the lesson.

Skills

1. Locating and applying word origins and meanings
2. Writing romance in the medieval style
3. Recognizing and using inference
4. Developing characterization
5. Using plot to focus narrative
6. Refining oral and written presentation skills

Concepts

1. Medieval romance as a genre of literature
2. The function of legends as stories of larger-than-life people
3. The human need to create to literature
4. Chivalry as a way of life
5. The relationship of a hero to society
6. Human life as a constant struggle for meaning

Assessment

1. Student and teacher evaluation of students' writing based on mutually established individual goals
2. Student self-assessment based on journal entries, including the final "What I learned . . ."
3. Student and teacher assessment of presentations—written, oral, interpretive, artistic
4. Teacher assessment of affective skills throughout the cooperative work
5. Teacher and student assessment of affective goals, especially in the area of effort, on the culminating activity (English highlights are presented in Figure 4–7)

FIGURE 4–7   English Highlights: The Medieval World—Anything but the Dark Ages

Focus Points	Facts	Skills	Concepts
1. Cultural development	1. Literary terms such as *myth, legend,* and *folktale*	1. Locating and applying word origins and meanings	1. Relationship of the hero to society
2. Power of the Church	2. Poetry terminology	2. Using inference	2. Legends' function in creating models
3. Organizational structures	3. People and characters from readings	3. Developing characterization in writing	3. Medieval romance as a genre of literature

Sample Activities:

1. As an advance organizer, students will brainstorm, categorize, and classify the abstract qualities of a hero. Using this material, students will write a short paper defining *hero.*

2. Students will read myths of King Arthur that emphasize aspects of the hero.

3. Students will study poetry and songs of the era, noting figures of speech, tone, mood, and theme. Students will compose and present original work to the class.

THE SOCIAL STUDIES CLASS FOCUS

Materials

1. World History text

2. Atlas

3. Supplementary readings

4. Student-created maps and charts

5. Teacher-prepared supplementary readings

Activities and Time

1. Week 1 is a time for the overview of the Middle Ages and for activating student knowledge and involvement through an advance organizer.

    a. The advance organizer is a two-day activity. The class is divided into five groups, which analyze five questions and prepare their answers in some form of graphic organizer. On the first day, students ponder the questions. The second day is for presentation, comparison, discussion, and making connections to the medieval period. The areas and questions are as follows:

        •   *Loyalty:* What does the term mean? To whom do we owe loyalty? The Romans were expected to show loyalty. To whom or what? Why?

        •   *Legal system:* What is the difference between having a set of written laws and such tests as trial by ordeal or trial by combat?

        •   *Literacy and common language:* What would happen to us as a society if we were to lose our books and have our schools and universities dismantled? How could we begin to rebuild such a system?

- *The town:* What purpose does a town serve? How is a town used for both trade and administration?
- *Religion:* What is the role and value of religion in society?

b. As homework throughout the week, students work on finding definitions and explanations for key vocabulary (people, events, documents, decisions) of the period. This is assessed through a test on Friday. A few minutes each day are spent quickly verifying definitions.

c. Additionally, students complete assigned readings that give them a general overview and a foundation of knowledge about Middle Ages for the next weeks' activities. After each reading, students write a one-page reaction paper. As a final activity to the readings, students, working in cooperative groups, create illustrated time-lines listing dates for the major events, people, and places of the age. These charts are posted throughout the room and used as reminders and activators for discussion.

2. Week 2 is to examine the composition and function of the feudal system, daily life on the manor, daily life in the monastery, and the effects of the system as a whole on the various levels within the system.

a. For the first three days of the week, students, working in groups, research and design charts, schemata, diagrams, and models of the manor, the monastery, castles, cathedrals, and the organizational structures holding the society together. Depending on the size of the class, additional groups can be formed to prepare a demonstration of the various types of armor and weapons, an illustrated chart listing elements of the chivalric code, and another chart on heraldic symbols and designs.

b. During the final two days of the week, the students present and explain their final products to the class. Written materials are submitted for a grade. Additionally, students complete a take-home test.

3. The third week is devoted to a study of the Black Death. During this week, students spend two days researching the plagues that struck Europe during this period. Students draw maps, create charts of the numbers and percentages involved, and draw inferences about the effect of this high number of deaths on a society. On the third and fourth days, students present their information to the class and plan the final activity of the week. On Friday, to draw attention to the impact of plagues and disease throughout the day, students ask selected members of the school to wear red ribbons symbolizing that the wearer has died of a plague. At the end of the day, on the final PA announcements, students from the World History classes will read a brief statement about the number and percentage of people who died during the day, and the time frame the day actually represented. This will make a strong connection for students to see that plagues and diseases were not only a fear of the Middle Ages. (This can easily be adapted to include an AIDS awareness program within the school.)

4. The fourth week is time for the Crusades. Again, group work and activity are the focus points. Students are assigned work groups, each of which concentrates on one of the following areas: one of the four Crusades, the overall effect of the Crusades, or the conditions in Europe that fostered the Crusades. Students have two days to research their topics and another day to prepare their maps, charts, and organizers for class presentations. During the final two days of the week, students demonstrate and explain. As well as submitting the written materials and charts, students complete a two-page paper on the causes and effects of the Crusades.

5. Week 5 is invention week. A number of significant inventions occurred during the Middle Ages. Students, working either in pairs or individually, are given two days of class time to research and find inventions that they can construct. Construction occurs outside of class. The next few days should be spent in planning the medieval festival with the English class. The students should have the weekend to put the finishing touches on their inventions. On Monday, students demonstrate their inventions and describe the purpose of each and its effect on society. Additionally, each student submits a written paper on the invention.

6. Week 6 is the time to look at the growth of towns, cities, and nations. Students are assigned to cooperative work groups to research the events and situations that occurred sequentially, giving rise to towns, cities, and eventually nations. Students should discover things such as food production, demand for goods, trade, economic system, technology, personnel needed and created by growth, the rise of the middle class, guilds, and administration or government. Groups are given two days to research and two days to create an imaginary town which they present to the class on Friday. Each group should design organizers to show structures, a map of their town, and key places. Students also write a one- to two-page paper on the growth of the town and its impact on the society of the Middle Ages.

7. Week 7 is dedicated to an analysis of the Magna Carta and to assigning roles and duties for the approaching festival. On day 1, the class reads an essay about the Magna Carta, which students will break down into key points about the conditions in England that led to the document. On the second day, they analyze the major changes and draw inferences about the impact of such change on the society. Students write a one-page reaction to the issues discussed in class. The remainder of the week is spent in preparation of the festival.

8. Week 8 is filled with specific preparations for the festival, which ideally is held on Friday of that week to bring a neat closure to the unit.

Total Time: 8 weeks

Factual Material

The factual material in this unit is long and is concerned primarily with people, places, dates, events, inventions, battles, and countries that are important to the era.

Skills

1. Creating timelines
2. Cartography
3. Creating graphic organizers to explain material
4. Reading charts
5. Separating fact from opinion
6. Researching and documenting material
7. Manipulating facts and statistics to use in presentations

Concepts

1. Religion as an organizational structure in the Middle Ages
2. Events in history as reactions to other events
3. How the relationship of environment and human needs creates a town
4. Technological advancements and their impact on the society.
5. How meeting basic needs determines the quality of human lives
6. Entertainments as a reflection of the culture

Assessment

1. Student self-evaluation based on mutually determined goals
2. Peer evaluation of group work and presentations
3. Teacher evaluation of oral and written presentation and documentation
4. Teacher evaluation of activity achievement
5. Student mastery of specified facts and skills
6. Teacher assessment of affective skills throughout the cooperative work
7. Teacher and student assessment of affective goals, especially in the area of effort, on the culminating activity (social studies highlights are presented in Figure 4–8)

FIGURE 4–8   Social Studies Highlights: The Medieval World—Anything but the Dark Ages

Focus Points	Facts	Skills	Concepts
1. Growth of cities and nations	1. Dates	1. Separating fact from opinion	1. Religion as an organizational structure
2. Historical events	2. People	2. Manipulating facts and statistics in presentations	2. Relationship of environments and needs to growth of towns
3. Inventions	3. Events	3. Researching and documenting material	3. Acquisition of basic needs to determine quality of life

Sample Activities:

1. Students will complete an advance organizer identifying key ideas and concepts of the Middle Ages such as loyalty, literacy, and purposes of towns. As they complete each idea, they will create and post a chart outlining elements.

2. Students will research types of plagues and their effect on Europe. This activity will culminate in a "death day" when students will ask members of the student body to wear ribbons signifying their death from a plague. This will graphically portray the scope of devastation.

3. Students will select and design major inventions from the Middle Ages. This will be demonstrated to the full class.

COMMON LINKAGES

Materials

1. Student-generated work (writings, charts, organizers)

2. Texts used in each class

3. Supplementary readings

4. Videotapes of any presentations

5. Teacher-supplied supplementary readings and activities

Activities and Time

The medieval festival is the culminating event of the unit. As the classes worked their way through the unit, a number of activities have already occurred that should be included in the fair. However, there are still activities that need to be addressed specifically for the fair.

1. "Who am I?" Each student should have a role for the fair, drawn from either the history or the literature of the time. On the basis of their research and reading, students will assume the persona of the character and remain in character throughout the fair. Possible characters include Merlin, King Arthur, Robin Hood, King John, monks, bards, jongleurs, troubadours, and so on. The more varied the characters, the better. Coordination will prevent needless repetition of roles.

2. The fair can be divided into three segments: booths and entertainments, a tournament, and the banquet. In this way, all facets of the Middle Ages can be presented.

3. Organization: Students should be in groups that include members from each class to organize the logistics of the event. A student chairperson should be appointed from each class to coordinate activities. Functioning in small groups, students need to establish location, a plan of the area, a time sequence, a place for props, a method for handling food storage, a stage manager, and a cleanup crew.

4. Each student writes a three- to four-page paper on the full experience of the unit. They should emphasize the skills they have gained and the concepts they believe they have acquired from the Middle Ages study. Additionally, they should assess the affective criteria through their continued efforts and the final presentation.

Skills

1. Role playing a character

2. Working cooperatively to plan and implement a large-scale demonstration

3. Constructing a setting

4. Designing and making costumes

5. Blending fact and fiction

6. Creating charts, displays, and organizers

7. Learning to budget time efficiently

8. Linking knowledge with personal experience

Concepts

1. The interrelationship of literature and history

2. How involvement creates knowledge

3. Human beings as the products of their environment

4. The influence of elements of culture on the level of human need

Assessment

1. Teacher and student assessment of the festival

2. Teacher reaction and evaluation of student papers on the unit

3. Teacher assessment of students' mastery of mutually determined goals (interdisciplinary highlights are presented in Figure 4–9)

FIGURE 4–9   Interdisciplinary Activities: The Medieval World—Anything but the Dark Ages

Interdisciplinary Objectives	Shared Skills	Shared Concepts
1. Developing frameworks for presenting and sharing information	1. Character role play	1. The close relationship of literature and history
2. Developing skills to differentiate between fact and fiction, myth and reality	2. Blending fact and fiction	2. How involvement creates knowledge
3. Developing cooperative work skills	3. Learning to budget time	3. How level of human need is influenced by events of culture

Activities: Medieval Festival

1. "Who am I?" Each student will assume a role for the festival and stay in character.

2. Students will create booths, entertainment, and competitions.

3. Students will write a three- to four-page paper explaining what they learned through creating and participating in the festival.

CONCLUSIONS

The medieval unit can be an invigorating and exciting experience for both teachers and students. It demands the continual interaction of the teachers, but it allows each teacher initially to introduce and refine subject-specific materials and themes. As students progress through the activities, it offers a number of areas for mutual work to occur. Furthermore, it allows teachers to function in two different areas while exploring the period of time. In addition, the unit offers a number of areas in which teachers can establish common themes to foster connections between the classes.

Themes such as the quest can certainly be examined through the Crusades and the literary Holy Grail. The theme of survival readily applies to the serfs on the manor, the knights in the Crusades, and the men of Sherwood Forest. Heroism is found in many areas of the literature and can certainly be applied to people battling the plague or fighting in the Crusades, and in the tales of the knights of the Round Table. The theme of nature is powerful in the lives of the peasants, in its role in some of the inventions, and in its influence on the medieval songs and poetry. The search for values is reflected not only in the knights and morality of King Arthur but also in the nobleman who stood up to King John and demanded a Magna Carta.

The Middle Ages are an ideal era to study using activities as the central style of learning. Additional activities that could be adapted to the unit include students making armor, producing a morality play, writing a Canterbury Tale, constructing their own castles and cathedrals, or conducting a medieval university class. Many of these activities can even be constructed so that they can be used in either or both classrooms. Learning is not the sole property of one discipline or the other—it belongs to all. The more the activities are shared, the greater the learning for the students.

A Note about Resources

Many of the materials that are needed for this exercise are found in many schools. The World History textbook provides a good overview and beginning point. For many of the activities, library resources are needed. We have emphasized the importance of the librarian and the library for this type of activity. Because it is virtually impossible for the individual departments to have all the resources needed for so comprehensive a unit, it is imperative that library resources are available to teachers during class time as well as before and after school.

There are various resources that can make planning an activity-based unit easier. To share a few, the Higgins Armory Museum of Worcester, Massachusetts, offers "Picture the Middle Ages," a wealth of experiential information and sound advice on creating some artifacts and banquets of the era. Additionally, the Then and There Series on The Medieval World from Longman Press is readable and manageable for students. *Scholastic Scope Magazine* in November 1981 and January 1993 offered interesting and colorful adaptations on the Arthurian legends and materials at varying reading levels.

Final Comments

This unit can make believers out of teachers who are still struggling with the issues of interdisciplinary work. From the teachers' point of view, it is comprehensive and cooperative. From the students' point of view, it is fun and engaging. *Fun* is important in the classroom. Students love big projects that offer a chance to escape from the confines of the classroom into another era. This unit offers possibilities for involving the whole school or certain selected groups in the festival. It would be an inexpensive field trip for elementary students, who would provide a great audience. Scheduling can be adapted for a full day, a half day, late afternoon, or early evening. The options are as numerous as the activities. From our experiences, students have thoroughly enjoyed the activities of this medieval unit while learning the important lessons synthesizing the whys, hows, and effects that various events, decisions, and people have on shaping life during an era.

UNIT-LENGTH THEMES

Title:	Transitions
Subject Areas:	Sociology and English
Ages/Grades:	Grade 12
Number of Students:	20–40
Focus Points:	1. How we learn to pass through the significant points of transition in our lives
	2. The experience of maturing given the societally imposed change in late adolescents
Time Necessary:	One quarter (8–10 weeks)

OVERVIEW

High school seniors face one of the turning points in life that society imposes on all of us. It is truly a time of *transition.* For some, it is a time of emotions running the gamut from extreme joy to deep sorrow. For most, it is a time filled with ritual and tradition.

This unit offers the teachers of senior students the opportunity to capitalize on what is influencing those students. The unit *connects* the transition students are facing directly with a classroom topic. Learning thus becomes more than something separated from reality. Instead, it becomes what is being lived at the moment as well as something occurring in the classroom. In the best use of resources, the school becomes the laboratory for the classroom.

Senior year of high school is an exciting time, a time of passion and energy. But it is also a volatile time in that students, often for the first time, are asked to make choices in a formal and public manner. Some schools have yearbooks, complete with memories and "future plans" sections. At other schools, students are featured in local newspapers. Occasionally, graduating students are included in brief television spots.

Seniors are often asked, "What are you doing next year?" in a chorus of curious voices. For some, the voices get more specific and ask, "What school are you going to go to?" Later still, the same voices often ask, "Where did you get into?" Finally, the last word is, "Where are you going?"

While students are living through this process, and schools involve them in rituals associated with graduation, being a senior, and worrying about "who will make it," classrooms remain unconnected places where someone else's fact often takes the place of the student's reality. Some classrooms do connect to the issues seniors face, but often *they* are not connected to other *classrooms.* These connections may well be taking place in a few schools, but from our experience and what others tell us, this is not the rule. What's missing is often a concerted effort to turn the experience of seniors into the focus of classroom experience and to link that experience to a dual view of the process of passing from one stage of life to the next. At the senior high level, as we graduate students, we should be creating interdisciplinary activity that is geared to meeting *student needs,* not focusing on meeting the demands of a curriculum. This is the time for interdisciplinary activity based on a common theme and common threads of student experience.

More often than not, teaming of teachers takes place at the middle or junior high school level. Those students are seen as having a "common" need. A case can easily be made for those students who are at the last step of the senior high school. These students share a common interest and common dilemmas, although not all will choose the same outcome. Likewise, their teachers share similar populations and have an opportunity to work with each other and with a *similar group* of students in creating curriculum that focuses on what is common rather than what is different. This unit offers an interdisciplinary strategy that links students and teachers around the common theme of *transitions*. It includes contributions and expectations from both groups. At the same time, it is flexible and should be adapted as an *outline* and a *framework* by others to meet their needs.

Within this model, we list the facts, skills, and concepts that constitute what can be added to a thematic study from the curricula of Sociology and English. We also present a list of activities that can be used and address some nuts-and-bolts considerations.

The students constituting our classroom group represent a diversity of learners. There is no one group of students selected for the class, nor are students in the class on the basis of evaluative criterion. The activities that follow are designed directly to foster collaboration as well as personal self-discovery and achievement.

INTERDISCIPLINARY OBJECTIVES

1. Students will work on developing higher level thinking skills associated with analyzing information.

2. Students will experience gathering information from a variety of sources and using that information in reflective activities.

3. Students will work cooperatively on collaborative research.

4. Students will recognize the impact of commonly shared experiences on a group such as a class.

5. Students will be able to develop an appreciation for the power of socially constructed transitions.

6. Students will be presented with the concept of a *life cycle* and how that idea is interconnected with concepts in literature and social science.

INTRODUCTION

In this unit, which lasts an average of eight to ten weeks, or about one-quarter of the school year, a Sociology class and an English class examine the way a culture organizes passages from one level of social life to the next. Detailed focus is given to the process of passage, along with corresponding symbolic rituals (graduation, future plans) that high school seniors are living through.

A central point in the unit is the ability of the English and social studies teachers to parallel each other's teaching at times, to use other time for instruction geared to a specific discipline, and at other times to bring the classes together for common activity.

THE SOCIOLOGY CLASS FOCUS

Materials

1. Sociology text
2. Teacher-supplied readings
3. Student-created survey

Activities and Time

1. Teacher presentation and classroom discussion of sociological subject matter dealing with socialization and the life cycle continue throughout the unit.

2. Students compile a chart of the rituals associated with high school graduation. The social and personal dimensions of each school and societal ritual are noted. This work is done in work groups of four students. It should be completed in two days during the first week of the unit.

3. Students compile a chart of the stereotypes associated with high school graduation and the impact of those stereotypes on personal behavior. This work is done in work groups of four students and should be completed in one day during the first week.

4. Students write a short paper (three pages) explaining how the graduation process can be seen as a sociological phenomenon. It is due at the end of the second week.

5. Students design a small-scale survey dealing with senior perceptions of their school years, and administer the survey to the senior class (or a random sample of the class). Survey design takes place during week 3. The survey is administered at week's end. This survey could provide the starting point for a continuing effort of a school to gain data on its community by sampling community members as they leave.

6. During week 4, students, working as a cooperative research group, conduct a basic descriptive statistical analysis of responses to the survey. Analysis to take place.

7. Students read two comparison articles provided by the teacher, that highlight the effects of age and passage in other cultures. Students read and discuss these articles in groups of three and highlight their responses with the other groups in class.

8. Students complete a take-home examination at the end of the unit.

Factual Material

Socialization, stereotypes, roles, transitions, culture, norms, self, game, play, taking the role of another, role distance, adolescence, peers, peer group, ritual, mean, median, mode

Skills

1. Collaborative work

2. Elementary data analysis

3. Survey coding and recording

4. Writing in the framework of a discipline

Concepts

1. The social forces that influence life passages

2. The ways social forces can affect the lives of individuals

3. The similarities among members of a group, such as a senior class, in responding to change

4. The cultural rituals that link age to changes in social status

Assessment

1. Student self-assessment

2. Teacher assessment of student-produced work

3. Teacher assessment of student papers

4. Teacher assessment of take-home exam

5. Student group and peer assessment of involvement and contribution in activities (sociology class focus is presented in Figure 4–10)

FIGURE 4–10   Sociology Highlights: Transitions

Focus Points	Facts	Skills	Concepts
1. Having students use the experience of transitions as a vehicle for classroom and self-learning	1. Knowledge of various sociological terms	1. Collaborative group work	1. Understanding the process of social passages
2. Students' recognition of the societal forces shaping their lives	2. Knowledge of the meanings suggested by various terms associated with social research	2. Survey coding and recording	2. The impact of transitions
3. Students' developing awareness of the issues raised by the field of sociology	3. Definitions of culture	3. Elementary data analysis	3. The importance of shared experience

Sample Activities:

1. Students will identify stereotypes through critical analysis of presented materials.

2. Students will write to explain sociological forces.

3. Students will conduct a small-scale survey.

148

THE ENGLISH CLASS FOCUS

Materials

1. Eight short stories related to the issue of adolescent passages and responses to change

2. Teacher-generated material

Activities and Time

1. The teacher provides an overview of representations of social transition in literature and the use of characterization in literature about entering adulthood.

2. Students read one short story during each of the eight weeks of this unit. The short stories deal with adolescents and young adults in *transition,* particularly the transition at the end of high school. The stories should include as wide a representation as possible of the various elements involved in the experience of transition. Students respond to each story with a short paper.

3. Students work for two days each week in discussion/reading groups of four and graphically represent themes within the stories they are reading.

4. For one day during each week, students work in groups of four to focus on the representation of characters and how they deal with uncertainty as they face transition. Students graphically organize the experiences of the characters in the stories and share their analysis with the class.

5. Students write a short story, preferably in the third person, which is turned in at the end of the class.

Factual Material

Characterization, specific characters in the short stories, irony, tragedy, comedy, satire, illusion, elements of a short story, plot, character, theme, setting, point of view

Skills

1. Critical reading and thinking

2. Cooperative and collaborative group work skills

3. Writing focused on reflection

4. Graphic representation of thoughts

5. Creative writing

Concepts

1. The use of transition as a topic in literature to gain access to universal experience

2. The role of uncertainty in literature about entering adulthood

3. The importance of developing characters in dealing with an individual's responses to change

4. The tension between an individual's response to transition and the demands of the group and society

Assessment

1. Peer response to student group work

2. Teacher evaluation of student papers

3. Student self-assessment

4. Teacher evaluation of student class and group work

5. Teacher and student evaluation of student-written short stories (English class highlights are presented in Figure 4–11)

FIGURE 4–11 English Highlights: Transitions

Focus Points	*Facts*	*Skills*	*Concepts*
1. Study of contemporary literature	1. Characters from specific stories	1. Critical reading and thinking	1. The idea of universal experience represented by literature
2. Linking personal experience with works of fiction	2. Specific elements found in all stories	2. Writing focused on reflection	2. The role of uncertainty in life
3. Viewing transitions in life as a universal experience communicated through literature	3. Elements specific to particular short stories	3. Analysis of literature	3. The idea of transition as a form of struggle

Sample Activities:

1. Students will read short stories as individuals and as members of a group.

2. Students will write short stories.

3. Students will engage in developing an analysis of short stories.

150

COMMON LINKAGES

Materials

1. Student-generated material (interviews)
2. Student-generated material (diaries)
3. Popular film about transition after high school
4. Video documentary about life after high school

Activities and Time

1. All students making up the same population in both classes are required to conduct one interview focusing on five questions generated within the class. Interviews are conducted with other members of the senior class. The aim is to interview as many of the seniors, graduating or not, as possible. If there are not enough people in the English–Sociology group to interview all members of the class, interviews are assigned on the basis of a randomly selected list of subjects. The interviews are audiotaped and transcribed in a typed format. They are based on a general list of five to eight questions students generate in a one-day class dedicated to interviews and interviewing. Students have the entire span of the unit to complete their interviews, which are due at the beginning of the last week of the unit. The interviews, transcribed as anonymous reports, then serve as the centerpiece for small-group analysis and reporting by students. The transcripts of the interviews serve a second purpose; they are donated to the school as part of its history, to be added to in future years.
2. All students are required to complete daily journals relating their experiences in both classrooms to what they are experiencing as they and their peers deal with the demands of transition.
3. The final results of the questionnaire are circulated to all students to provide an opportunity for original individual, group, and class analysis.
4. The information students generate is used to frame the experience of writing a short story.
5. A final activity brings together all students to construct a number of themes common to their collective experience as seniors in high school.

Skills

1. Designing an interview
2. Conducting an interview and transcribing the results for presentation to others
3. Organizing and writing a journal
4. Working cooperatively and collaboratively in a group
5. Conducting a critical analysis of interviews
6. Creative writing

Concepts

1. Addressing the idea of transition through two separate areas of study
2. The unanticipated demands transitions place on those living through them
3. Compromise as an important element in coping with transition
4. Transitions, such as the end of the high school experience, that are shared by large numbers of people

Assessment

1. Teacher reaction to journals
2. Teacher assessment of interviews
3. Student self-response to interviews
4. Student assessment of group work designed to analyze interview transcripts (interdisciplinary highlights are presented in Figure 4–12)

FIGURE 4–12   Interdisciplinary Activities: Transitions

Interdisciplinary Objectives	Shared Skills	Shared Concepts
1. Developing higher level thinking skills through analyzing information	1. Designing an interview	1. Addressing the idea of transition through two subject areas
2. Recognizing the impact of a commonly shared experience on a group	2. Organizing and writing a journal	2. The many issues integrated in understanding transitions
3. The concept of the "life cycle"	3. Conducting an interview and transcribing the results	3. Transitions as social constructions

Sample Activities:

1. Students will be required to complete an interview of a peer.
2. Students will complete a daily journal.
3. Students will either complete an outline or write their own short story based on themes they have identified through their journals and research.

SUMMARY

This unit offers a rare opportunity to link experiences not only with one subject area but with two. It provides a dual focus to a common theme linked to what we encounter as human beings. By the end of the unit, students have become the creators of the material framing their academic pursuit. It is their background, tempered with views from social science and from literature, that becomes the driving force and leads them to self- and critical inquiry.

This type of unit becomes new each time it is taught in that the underlying forces linking the two subject areas frame themes that are not linked to a specific year or a specific place. Yet, for all the students participating in the activity, these themes are, in fact, linked to a particular time and place. The unit is also open enough to be modified to fit other issues of transition. The passage into adulthood requires learning to deal with many new roles, not simply that of a graduate. Any one of these roles, as it is experienced by students in junior and senior high schools and is age-appropriate, would thematically organize a unit and could be approached through two disciplines.

A Note about Resource Material

The model presented here provides the openness and flexibility for teachers to use the resources they choose. As the section on the sociology class indicates, a textbook can be used if the instructor wishes. Likewise, the teacher can find articles describing transitions in other cultures from a variety of sources including (but not limited to) periodicals (such as *National Geographic*), anthropology journals, and material in the popular press, both magazines and newspapers.

The English teacher has an equal amount of leeway in finding material that is appropriate for senior high school students and fits the theme of transition. There are a myriad of short stories available for a teacher to use. The stories of Joyce Carrol Oates, which often deal with the lives of young Americans, come to mind, but there are many other rich literary sources as well.

Some Hints and Notes

This unit can provide opportunities for teaming and for team teaching. Each individual activity can take place in separate classrooms or in the same classroom, with two teachers or with one. Teachers contemplating such a unit might try to schedule back-to-back classes with the same group of students. Although this may seem impossible at first glance, it is often a practical solution. To include more than one section of an English class with most of the students also engaged in a sociology class may be an acceptable modification.

Students can design a thirty-item questionnaire about aspects of school life. Similarly, they can create an interview guide consisting of five to ten open-ended questions that will enable them to conduct an interview with a peer. Issues of anonymity and ethics will need to be addressed. Also, the teacher must be willing to work as a guide rather than telling students what to ask. Students usually respond with enthusiasm to this research task because they have a sense of "ownership" of the project. After all, the research is about themselves and what they are living through. It gives them a strong grounding on which to base their own short stories.

This unit emphasizes collaborative and collective work on the part of students and teachers. (The charts we have included, highlighting this, can be used as guides.) There is a sense of working together at both the practical day-to-day level and the broader intellectual level. For example, at times when both classes need to come together, particularly at the end of the unit, the issue of space will need to be addressed. Again, this is an obstacle that is easily overcome. At other times, students as class members or group members will need to *think together*. They must find a way to draw conclusions

153

that contribute to an analysis of the material that they, their peers, and their teachers generate.

For all this to happen, two teachers must come together and draw up a set of common plans. There must be agreement, coordination, and mutual respect between the teachers in order to create a symmetry in which each subject area complements the other. There must also be a balance within each subject area in which the material generated by the teacher honors and includes on an equal footing the material created by students.

UNIT-LENGTH THEMES

Title:	The Individual and the State: A Trial
Subject Areas:	English and Law
Ages/Grades:	Grade 11
Number of Students:	18
Focus Points:	1. The connection of the ideas of the law and of literature
	2. How fictional societies use the law
	3. The relationship between our society and fictional societies
	4. The use of the trial process in society
Time Necessary:	1 quarter (approximately 10 weeks)

OVERVIEW

This unit offers students in a team-taught class the opportunity to use the work of a social studies course focusing on law related education and that of an English class to construct a knowledge base that complements each discipline. It builds on the strengths of two subject areas while allowing students to create new and individualized understandings of the law as used in the trial process and of a work of twentieth-century literature.

Specifically, students will read George Orwell's *1984* and will be asked either to defend or to prosecute the character Winston Smith on a charge of treason. In this unit, an English teacher addresses Orwell's *1984* as a literary work, while a social studies teacher addresses the topic of the trial process as it relates to the U.S. Constitution and our system of law. After a period of combined study, students conduct a mock trial. This activity serves as the endpoint of the unit.

Orwell's *1984* holds an enormous impact both as a work of literature and for its prophetic social commentary. It addresses issues that have become paramount in our world of today. The idea of the power of the state continues to hold the attention of the world. It suggests understandings that all students should appreciate, for they are the ones who will have to deal with the realities of the state, whether in their own nation or in dealing with other nations.

The trial process is one of the building blocks of our society in the way we organize relationships. It provides us a mechanism to settle disputes with one another and with the state. Yet too often students whose only experience with the process comes from television or from a personal involvement with the court system ignore the importance of the process. A mock trial involves students in their learning (for a greater description of how trials can be used in the classroom, see Nowicki & Meehan, 1996). It brings the facts of a trial to life as students become participants in the process. The mock trial format encourages cooperative effort on the part of the students; one of the strengths of the unit is in bringing students to a recognition of the importance of collaboration in attaining success. Similarly, students learn through participation in the trial process that cooperative efforts lead to cooperative strengths that originate in the individual contributions made to the group as it seeks to resolve a problem.

This unit contains the notion of competition, on which the trial process is based. Students are asked by their peers to be prepared, to understand Orwell's work from the perspective of a character, and to translate that perspective to a new context such as a mock court. In many situations, competition can be a healthy component of the teaching/learning process. It can add a sense of team and responsibility while involving students. Competition is healthy as long as students have input into the situation and realize clearly the objective of the activity. If *individual responsibilities* are *clearly* stated at the beginning of the activity and if the *outcomes* and *expectations* are also made *explicit* and *clear,* students will respond.

This unit demands that two teachers work together and maintain open lines of communication. Teachers must plan together and divide time between them to enhance the common purpose of prompting students to explore, create, and learn. Team teaching can be the most rewarding of experiences or the most devastating. Teachers need to respect each other and learn to work closely together without fear of destructive rather than creative comment. We have been in team teaching situations, and we appreciate the level of professional trust that must develop before two teachers can successfully undertake such an endeavor. Teachers need to feel free to disagree in their work and in listening to each other's work. In other words, they need to communicate and collaborate rather than maintain a sense of superiority. All these attributes are what we would expect our students to develop and must begin with the work of teachers, who are the models for students.

INTERDISCIPLINARY OBJECTIVES

1. Students will come to an understanding of the forces that shape our daily life as it relates to the security a system of government provides.

2. Students will come to a better understanding of the duality of purpose inherent in the learning process as they understand the detail and various levels of a literary work through use of the trial process and related law.

3. Students will be given evidence to help them understand the tension that exists in the relationship of chaos and order.

4. Students will arrive at a personally constructed definition of totalitarianism.

5. Students will conduct research collaboratively.

6. Working on teams, students will cooperatively demonstrate information they have gained through individual, group, and class effort.

INTRODUCTION

This unit consists of a *team-taught* class that lasts from eight to ten weeks, or one quarter of the school year. It can be a first component of a half-year course (offering a separate mock trial during the second quarter) or just a one-quarter course in schools that follow a quarterly schedule. An English teacher and a social studies teacher combine their strengths in this unit as they help students pursue a study of human experience through literature and law. Students are asked to place the character Winston Smith on trial for treason. The mock trial provides the framework for the unit and its summary activity. Students assume the roles of various characters from Orwell's *1984*. Some of the characters are assigned to the defense and some to the prosecution. Additionally, four students are assigned to the roles of attorney for the state and four are designated defense attorneys. Other students are assigned to class-created roles such as the judge and the arresting officer.

This mock trial format (described in detail in Nowicki & Meehan, 1996) is used as a vehicle to get at what students create as the truth of the literary work. Although the trial format is similar to that of the U.S. system of justice, it is modified by both teachers to meet the needs of their students. For example, students serving on the prosecution and defense teams deliver opening and closing statements and conduct direct and cross-examinations. Students serving as witnesses become the characters they represent. The case is tried before a jury selected by the teachers from the school's population. Objections are allowed for a limited number of reasons. One is failure to stay within the bounds of the text. Other objections are for asking leading questions during a direct examination, forcing relevant questions and testimony, and badgering witnesses.

Witnesses testify for a timed period set by the teachers and the class in working out the ground rules. For example, direct examinations can last seven minutes, while cross-examinations last only five. The same can be done for opening and closing statements. This type of activity is intentionally flexible to allow for as much modification as teachers and students deem necessary.

Although the entire work *1984* serves as an anchor of the course, we suggest that witnesses and other characters at the trial be allowed to use only information gleaned from Parts I and II. These parts make for an interesting case and limit the students to only a certain amount of admissible information.

THE LAW CLASS FOCUS

Materials

1. Text—law-related

2. Teacher-supplied readings

3. Student-produced written and graphically displayed materials

Activities and Time

1. After an overview provided by a teacher, during the first week of class, students spend two class days analyzing questions related to law as opposed to questions related to fact. Working in cooperative groups, they respond to information provided by a teacher about understanding the differences in these types of questions.

2. For three days, students study the Bill of Rights and the trial process. Working in pairs or groups of three, they are assigned one or two amendments from the Bill of Rights to study and report on to the rest of the

class. Students are given a question dealing with the Bill of Rights to help frame a reflective essay due at week's end. Material is provided by the text or is teacher-generated.

3. Students work for two days studying the topic of treason. In short readings (from the text or teacher-generated), students are presented with the issue of treason, why it is important for a society to consider, how societies have dealt with treason, and current laws regarding treason. At the end of the week, students, having worked in groups of three, provide the class with group definitions of treason and represent those definitions on charts and organizers. At the end of the week, students are to construct their responses to the group definition of treason in an essay.

4. Students receive an overview of a trial procedure. They spend two days learning the routine of opening and closing statements, what perjury means and how to conduct direct and cross-examinations of witnesses. Then they select their roles for the upcoming trial. Students are asked to provide examples of direct and leading questions based on a common experience within the class to practice on their peers. Teachers will collect these questions and return them with comments.

5. Working in groups representing the prosecution and the defense, respectively, students begin to prepare strategy for the mock trial. The roles of story characters and other players are assigned. This activity takes three class days. Students are given an individual take-home exam due at the end of the week summarizing questions of law covered during the first five weeks of the class.

6. In week 6, three days of law activity are devoted to all students, characters, attorneys, and others working on their respective team. The judge and teachers float between prosecution and defense. Students representing characters begin to write their statements for the court based on information from the story. Attorneys begin to write up drafts of questions to be used in direct examinations and in cross-examinations, as well as opening and closing statements. Statements are shared for commentary and editing with the individual's team. A final draft is due the end of week. At some point, Winston Smith is arrested.

7. Week 7 is devoted to students working with each other as they prepare the case. Final drafts of student statements are submitted to the court by way of the judge and may be viewed by opposing sides.

8. Students conduct a mock trial.

9. Students conclude the mock trial and begin assessment. They are required to arrive at group evaluations of trial participation and are given a final take-home exam that includes an element geared to individual assessment.

Factual Material

Bill of Rights, Constitution, treason, role of an attorney, the adversary system, opening statement, closing statement, direct and cross examination, the steps in a trial, leading questions, the arrest process.

Skills

1. Working collaboratively

2. Designing questions

3. Writing statements based on existing material

4. Conducting critical analysis

5. Participating in a group evaluation

Concepts

1. Understanding the difference between a question of law and a question of fact

2. Understanding why our courtrooms are based on the adversary system

3. Recognizing the purpose behind the steps in a trial

4. Understanding the use of leading questions

Assessment

1. Student self-assessment of participation in group activities

2. Student peer assessment of group work

3. Teacher assessment of written student work

4. Teacher assessment of student group work (law class highlights are presented in Figure 4–13)

FIGURE 4–13   Law Class: The Individual and the State: A Trial

Focus Points	Facts	Skills	Concepts
1. The use of the trial process	1. Bill or Rights and Constitution	1. Designing questions	1. Understanding the links and mutual support between law and social structures
2. The universality of law and rules in social life	2. Role of an attorney and the adversary system in the trial process	2. Writing statements	2. Understanding the adversary systems
3. The importance of the Bill of Rights	3. The trial process and steps in a criminal case	3. Group work and evaluation	3. Recognizing the reason for steps in the trial process

Sample Activities:

1. Students will work in groups studying questions of law as opposed to questions of fact.

2. Students will work in groups studying the Bill of Rights and the crime of treason.

3. Students will develop a prosecution and a defense for a mock trial.

THE ENGLISH CLASS FOCUS

Materials

1. George Orwell's *1984*

2. Teacher-generated materials

3. Student-produced materials

Activities and Time

1. During the first week of the class students begin a reading of *1984.* In groups, students focus on questions assigned by the teacher. These questions deal with issues such as the representation of life in the book and the impact of society on an individual. Groups report back to the full class for discussion. At the end of the first week students are assigned an individual written response.

2. During weeks two, three and four students continue to work in reading response groups which deal with teacher generated questions about character development and analysis of Orwell's novel. Students continue to respond at the end of the week in a written essay to the teacher generated questions and to the analysis conducted in the course of group work.

3. Weeks five and six find students in their trial groups. While they develop their knowledge of the first two parts of *1984* in preparation for the trial, they continue to read and analyze the final part of the book. They do in reading groups which reflect the distribution of students into prosecution and defense teams for the trial. Information gained from a study of this part of the book is not to be used as direct evidence for the trial.

4. Week 6 is directed toward an overview of Orwell, the literary and cultural flavor of the 1940s and of *1984*. This is presented by the teachers.

5. Week 7 is devoted to statement preparation, editing, and trial preparation.

6. During week 8 students conduct the mock trial.

7. Week 9 represents a time to evaluate the trial and to conclude thoughts on Orwell in relation to the world of today.

Factual Material

Elements of a story, plot, theme, setting, point of view, characterization, characters (who will be developed within the trial) such as Winston Smith, Tom Parsons, Julia, Katherine Smith, the old man, O'Brien, Mr. Charrington, Syme

Skills

1. Critical reading

2. Group work and processing

3. Writing for analysis

4. Translating a work of the past into situations in which it applies today

5. Critical thinking

Concepts

1. The struggle faced by people in society because of society.

2. Understanding the idea of a tragic hero. (Do we pity Winston? Would he want us to pity him?)

3. Understanding an author's point of view and the thesis underlying the meaning of the work.

4. The issue of emotion in terms of individuality and society.

Assessment

1. Teacher assessment of student group work

2. Teacher assessment of student responses to focus questions

3. Student self-assessment

4. Student peer assessment (highlights of English class are presented in Figure 4–14)

FIGURE 4–14   English: The Individual and the State: A Trial

Focus Points	Facts	Skills	Concepts
1. Connecting ideas of law and literature	1. Characters specific to the story of *1984*	1. Group work and processing	1. Understanding a thesis and the author's point of view
2. The relationship between actual and fictional societies	2. Analyzing elements of fictional stories	2. Writing for analysis	2. Understanding the idea *hero*
3. The use of law in fiction	3. Understanding the life of George Orwell	3. Critical thinking and critical reading	3. Recognizing the struggle imposed by society

Sample Activities:

1. Through the use of reading response groups, the class will study *1984.*

2. Students will prepare a mock trial.

3. Students will be involved in writing, peer editing, and generating a group product.

COMMON LINKAGES

Materials

1. *1984*

2. Student-generated materials

Activities and Time

1. Time is allocated during weeks 1 through 6 for both teachers to constantly connect through commonalities and differences offered through the perspectives of approaching *1984* legally and literarily. It is expected that both teachers share the review of all student work and offer individual responses to student generated work. It is essential teachers divide the class time into areas that offer the greatest common benefit and constantly reinforce the discussion and analysis taking place.

2. The interdisciplinary nature of this class is quite clear and closely follows the theme of *The Individual and the State*. During the last section of the class the contributions of interdisciplinary activity become paramount. The preparation and conduction of a mock trial highlight the interconnections and contributions of each perspective. Students will question Winston Smith, O'Brien, and others. They will struggle with deciding "what is treason?" in terms of the evidence presented. They will learn to understand the book at a number of complex levels and attempt to create meaning from an interdisciplinary exploration.

3. The mock trial should be videotaped for review by students and teachers at the end of the trial. It will be used by groups, individual students, and teachers as a focus point of assessment during the last week of the unit. Similarly, all student-generated material for the trial—including witness statements, attorney statements, all attorney questions, a judge's reaction, and descriptions of evidence (if any)—should be submitted at the end of the unit in a typed format and used to create a class book. The book is not only a collaborative work but also serves to provide another level and opportunity for assessment and, in the best sense of education, a lasting document for later classes to use as a resource. The final week will include a teacher-generated take home test.

    Please note the flow charts that are included at the end of this chapter.

Skills

1. Portraying characters

2. Doing group and collaborative work such as framing and presenting a group presentation and argument

3. Critical thinking in a collaborative frame of reference and translating thoughts into written work

4. Learning to construct a personal and peer assessment from a videotape of a long-term activity's product and from written documents submitted for the book

5. Self-editing and peer editing

6. Writing for an audience yet in a critical fashion

Concepts

1. The continuing struggle between order and chaos in society

2. Understanding the theme of the individual in the context of society

3. The singularity of perspectives offered by separate areas of study

Assessment

1. Student self-assessment of videotape and of trial experiences

2. Teacher assessment of mock trial

3. Student peer assessment of mock trial

4. Teacher and student assessment of materials generated for the class book

5. Teacher assessment of the final take-home test (interdisciplinary highlights are presented in Figure 4–15)

FIGURE 4–15 Interdisciplinary Activities: The Individual and the State: A Trial

Interdisciplinary Objectives	Shared Skills	Shared Concepts
1. Students will come to understand the security provided	1. Collaborative work in framing and presenting an argument	1. The struggle between order and chaos in society
2. Students will understand the relationship of order and chaos to social life	2. Self-assessment and peer assessment skills	2. The theme of the individual in the context of society
3. Students will create a definition of meaning of totalitarianism	3. Character portrayal	3. The singularity of perspectives offered by separate areas of study

Sample Activities:

1. Students will prepare and participate in a mock trial experience.

2. Students will build a group argument either for or against the actions of one of the characters.

3. Students will engage in a group and collaborative assessment activity.

SUMMARY

This unit offers an opportunity for teachers to come together and link their work to the needs of their students. In the ten-week study of Orwell's *1984* and the criminal trial system, a great deal more is experienced by students than would have been encountered in traditional English and social studies classes operating independently. Students in a traditional setting may have been exposed to a greater amount of factual material, but, through the mock trial activity, students gain a greater and deeper understanding of the skills and concepts that form the bulwark of the unit. This unit demonstrates alternatives adaptable to many schools. To be sure, such adaptations need the collaborative efforts of teachers, but the message is: *It can be done.*

What we have outlined here is flexible and open to modification. Teachers and students should be allowed to innovate and experiment with what we have suggested. For example, our model unit contains the roles for eight attorneys, four representing the defense and four representing the prosecution. It also includes roles for a student acting as a judge and for one acting as the arresting officer. Both roles are essential to the case. The arresting officer should make a formal arrest and not violate current existing standards of contemporary law. The judge needs to be well versed in making decisions that can impact a case and that are based on some sense of support. There is responsibility for learning what is expected of these roles. In the end it is *up to the student.* What better way to create ownership of knowledge?

Teachers and students may choose to follow the characters we mentioned—Winston Smith, O'Brien, Mr. Charrington, Syme, Tom Parsons, Katherine Smith, Julia, and the old man—or to vary the listing. Our trial uses eighteen students in a team-taught class. However, the option exists to create new roles or to subtract some based on the needs of the teacher and the class.

A Note about Resources and Materials

Most schools and English departments have access to *1984.* Most should also have some component stressing the law and law-related education. Teachers unsure about trial practices and procedures should go outside the school and ask an attorney from the community for volunteer assistance. The aim of this unit is to provide lessons that become ingrained and are reflected on years later, not overwhelming and fact-driven marathons of memory.

Our work with mock trials suggests that it is a strategy that is a resource in itself. They develop a sense of ownership about the knowledge they create.

There are glitches, and we need to share those as well as the success stories. For example, in a course that lasts two quarters, the first trial should carry a basic level of expectations. Students will make mistakes from which they can learn. The teacher, acting as responsible guide, should make sure that hard-working students are not singled out for a procedural or content mistake created in the process of a tense experience. We strongly believe students in the eleventh grade can effectively participate and learn from a mock trial experience. The students who take time to adjust in such a class are often those of high ability who have been long accustomed to relying on their own memory strength rather than their skills at cooperative analysis and self-critical thinking.

We have presented a unit that lasts a quarter but can serve as the beginning of a semester *interdisciplinary course.* For example, the second quarter can include a reading of two or three books, one of which becomes the centerpiece for the second mock trial. The only criterion is that the books must follow the theme of *the individual in relation to society in terms of the law.* There are many books that can fit. It is here that the two teachers can expand on the quality and quantity of learning they expect of their teaching and from their students. Our experiences tell us that students are receptive and take their cues from the actions of their teachers and schools.

There is one final resource and obstacle to address. Teachers are a resource, as are students. Unfortunately, as we mentioned earlier, schools, searching for cost-effectiveness, view two teachers in one classrooms with only eighteen or twenty students as a waste of people and space. This thinking agrees with the precepts of the bureaucratic model, but it is contrary to the models dedicated to offering quality education to all students. Some of our fondest memories of graduate-level education in the social sciences and in education, for example, were team-taught courses in which two instructors worked with a dozen or so students. Teachers in junior and senior high school need the opportunity to work together and to be rewarded for their work. Organizational structures and policy should reward these efforts rather than stifling them.

This unit offers many suggestions that can be worked into a curriculum and a school. All of them support the ideal of heterogeneous grouping and of bringing students together in ways that celebrate both the individual and the group. As with the other units in this section, students become owners of their intellectual efforts and constructions, through critical analysis from their learning.

UNIT-LENGTH THEMES

Title: Living in Other Cultures

Subject Areas: English and Social Studies (World Geography or World Cultures)

Ages/Grades: Grades 7 and 8

Number of Students: 20–100

Focus Points:

1. To connect students with the realities of living in another culture by studying the geography and life-styles found in another part of the world

2. To use the topic and content of studying another culture for learning social studies and English material

3. Forming a new government

4. To develop cooperative learning skills

Time Necessary: 6 weeks

OVERVIEW

This unit is unlike the other long units presented in this book because it does not deal with the senior high school level but is geared to junior high school students. In many ways, junior high schools are well on their way toward building interdisciplinary links and using themes to focus study. Many junior high schools have working teams of teachers that are assigned to specific groups of students. Others have initiated team teaching experiences across subject lines. Additionally, a number of junior high schools have either adopted heterogeneous grouping outright or are experimenting with innovations that utilize models based on mixed-ability classrooms. For example, in *Crossing the Tracks,* author Anne Wheelock tells us about many junior high schools that can serve as models for other schools shifting their organization from tracking.

There are reasons that junior high schools are often featured in the forefront of educational innovation. Having taught at both levels, we have found the atmosphere or climate different in junior high schools. Many seventh- and eighth-grade classes deal with collaborative instruction, others with hands-on activities and experiential learning. Still others have arranged the school day in ways that do not simply reflect a standard seven-period day. Our sense, derived from crossing the lines and teaching at both levels, is that there is a greater focus on process and on a child's social and emotional development rather than on the fact-driven curricula of senior high school classrooms. In many ways, junior high schools and teachers have much to showcase and model in terms of educational innovation for senior high school teachers.

Because there are educators in many junior high schools who are just beginning to look at the elimination of student and teacher tracking, it is important to include a sample unit aimed expressly at this area. Interdisciplinary units, defining ways for learning to be readapted, can help teachers and administrators meet the diversity of their students. Consequently, this unit

166

offers a strategy for linking the work of an English classroom with the activity of a social studies classroom. The six weeks we describe can lead to *parallel teaching, interdisciplinary activity* that reflects common interests for students, or *team teaching experiences.* Teachers are invited to adapt their materials and methodology to meet the needs of their colleagues and students at a pace and direction that the teachers select together.

To maintain the flexibility of the unit and keep it open to modification by the teacher, we do not list a specific content area other than English and Geography or World Cultures. However, we do offer examples of specific facts and concepts that are interdisciplinary and subject-linked. We also focus on subject-linked skills that are interdisciplinary and address the learning process. Junior high school is a place for skill development. It is a place where students can hone and perfect the skills that will facilitate access to information, spur creativity, and foster learning in later years. Within this unit, *teachers must identify those learning skills that are interdisciplinary and subject-specific.* In this way, a collaborative scope and sequence can be created emphasizing when the skills are to be introduced and reinforced. Once teachers have identified common skills, they then can work toward a collective criterion to assess skill mastery.

While a great deal of interdisciplinary crossover can be found in the content suggested by this unit, there remains a great deal within the province of English or social studies. This unit highlights those differences and celebrates the sense of diversity brought by teachers from different content backgrounds to the students in their classrooms. This unit does not advocate replacing English or social studies teachers with some newer model. It does tell us that their backgrounds and specialities are necessary in creating the medley of instructional strategies necessary for meeting the needs of mixed-ability classrooms.

For students, this unit offers a change to watch as teachers model collaborative behavior. It also provides a focus around a common theme that can impact the entire school, class, or grade. As a result, students will come to see their work in English and in social studies as focused on a common theme. The image of a theme is an important reinforcer for a seventh or eighth grader, although often the particular skills in the social studies or English class surrounding the topic may be quite different.

This model offers suggestions for many classroom teachers. Through adaptation, it can create new learning situations. It is also flexible enough that it can be adjusted to a number of schedule arrangements. Although it is presented as a junior high school unit, it does have a point of view that can be incorporated into a number of areas by senior high school teachers.

INTERDISCIPLINARY OBJECTIVES

1. Students will work on teacher-identified cognitive learning skills that connect English and social studies.

2. Highlighted criteria will indicate student mastery of interdisciplinary skills as teachers build an assessment model.

3. Through intra- and interdisciplinary group experiences, students will learn cooperative work skills and habits.

167

4. Students will recognize the unique features of a selected geographical culture area of the world.

5. Students will understand the importance of geography and culture in discerning the underlying diversity that exists among cultures.

6. Students will recognize the similarities that exist in many cultures.

7. Students will develop an appreciation for themselves as members of an interconnected world community and for the diversity that exists within the world community.

INTRODUCTION

This unit can last six weeks or longer, depending on the initial plans established by the teachers participating in the collaborative experience. For purposes of this unit description, we have focused on the East Asian geographic and culture region, although we emphasize that this unit could easily be shifted to another subject without altering the framework or the theme. The strategies can be text-based, based on other readings, or a combination of both. We leave the choice of what to use to the teacher. The suggested outlines follow a weekly sequence and provide time for subject area and interdisciplinary activity. The plans for each of the subject areas can be meshed into a complete interdisciplinary experience or can allow for teachers to team and parallel one another's work and bring students together for interdisciplinary activity.

THE SOCIAL STUDIES FOCUS

Materials

1. World Geography text (including culture regions of the world)

2. Student atlases

3. Additional readings

4. Videotaped features

5. Various encyclopedias, almanacs, and yearbooks

Activities and Time

1. Students begin a study of the East Asian culture region by drawing a map including countries, capitals, and other requirements listed by the teacher. They can use whatever they need, but maps are to be drawn *freehand*. Students are not graded on artistic ability but are assessed on their accuracy in locating listed items and on the amount of the list completed. This activity usually takes two to three days. Maps are then displayed in a gallery. The teacher also assigns terms to be researched and reading for homework during the week. A fourth day is dedicated to an enrichment activity and to reviewing each of the maps. The last day of the week is a test of geographical knowledge. Students may use the

maps they created.

2. The second week of the unit finds students engaged in building charts using large sheets of paper that contain information about the nations of East Asia. Teachers assign a list of topics, including literacy rates, life expectancy, major religions, populations, exports, imports, and GNP, among many others. Students locate information in reference material provided by the teacher. Students can prepare individual charts while working in groups or can create group charts. These charts serve as a resource throughout the unit and for a test at the end of the week. Teacher-prepared vocabulary is also included.

3. The third week is arranged around two topics: religions and languages. Working in groups, students are assigned a religion found in East Asia and are responsible for presenting information about the religion in a graphic report using group-designed posters. The teacher also adds material for reading.

4. Week 4 focuses on the economy of the region and continues to follow up on the information process initiated through work on the chart. Students are also encouraged to show the economic linkages of their society with that of East Asia.

5. During week 5, students, again working in groups, focus on the art, literature, and customs of East Asia. Again their reports are to utilize charts and graphs as well as individual essays.

6. Students work for the week in pairs or groups of three preparing for a class fair dedicated to presenting some item they find interesting about East Asia. Students should be encouraged to be as creative as they wish, and demonstrations should include all aspects of East Asian life, including music, art, and food.

Factual Material

Nations, capitals, oceans, seas, mountains, cities, languages, and populations; terms associated with types of music, art, religions, recreation, history, government, and other topics

Skills

1. Reading maps

2. Building charts

3. Researching topics

4. Contrasting and comparing cultures

5. Organizing and displaying information to others

6. Developing cooperative work skills

Concepts

1. Developing an awareness of the world's physical features

2. Understanding the relationship of economy to geography

3. Understanding the link between culture and geography

4. Viewing a chart as a profile of an area

5. Understanding the idea of interdependence

Assessment

1. Teacher assessment of maps, charts, and group work

2. Student assessment of maps, charts, and group work

3. Teacher assessment of student presentations

4. Student-written reactions to presentations (social studies highlights are presented in Figure 4–16)

FIGURE 4–16   Social Studies Highlights: Living in Other Cultures

Focus Points	Facts	Skills	Concepts
1. To connect students with the realities of life in another	1. Nations, capitals, and political entities	1. Understanding and reading maps	1. Understanding relationships such as geography and culture
2. To link geography with life style	2. Geographical features	2. Building charts and researching	2. Understanding the idea of interdependence
3. To develop cooperative group skills	3. Various cultural artifacts such as art, music, and language	3. Organizing and displaying information	3. Understanding the importance of diversity

Sample Activities:

1. Students will create maps, charts, and graphs of a specific cultural region.

2. Students will create graphic displays and posters of the art, music, and language of a region.

3. Students will work in groups toward demonstrating the knowledge they have gained to others.

THE ENGLISH CLASS FOCUS

Materials

1. One book for class (a work of fiction dealing with East Asia)

2. One book for home (dealing with the same topic; see notes for some suggestions)

3. Additional readings from magazines and newspapers

4. Video documentaries

Activities and Time

1. During this unit, students will read two books. The first will be a class activity lasting the first four weeks. It will be discussed in cooperative

reading discussion groups organized by the teacher. At the same time, students will be required to read a second book, which they select with the teacher's permission. For this book, the students will maintain a written journal with daily reactions to the book and to the knowledge gained about East Asia in general as it relates to their reading. At the same time, the teacher will focus the class on particular issues related to understanding the English language in a variety of writing assignments, geared toward the individual and the group.

2. Each week there will be a new set of vocabulary words assigned by the teacher. These words relate to linguistic operations, the book being read in class, or another class activity. These words will be used by students to write short essays geared to reactions, reports, or third-person narratives. An additional focus may be on a part of speech or type of word.

3. Students will engage in period-long activities during class time, which serve as additions to the in-class readings. For example, students might spend two days researching haiku in groups. This would culminate with individually produced haiku, which would be mounted on a chart circling the room.

4. Students work for the week in pairs or groups of three preparing for a class fair dedicated to presenting some interesting item about East Asia. Students should be encouraged to be as creative as they wish while preparing demonstrations which should represent all aspects of East Asian life, including music, art, and food.

Factual Material

Specific vocabulary words and terms associated with poetry and haiku

Skills

1. Analyzing written material

2. Writing critically

3. Writing for an audience

4. Writing poetry (haiku)

5. Translating words into picture (visually expressing haiku)

6. Using a growing vocabulary in speech and in writing

7. Using visual displays to demonstrate conclusions that students have drawn from what they have been experiencing

8. Developing cooperative work skills through group activity

9. Reading

10. Writing in the third person

Concepts

1. Books as a reflection of a language and a point of view

2. The idea of a writer's perspective and its relationship to culture

3. Language as an artifact of a culture that reflects the underlying beliefs of that culture

4. The universality of literature dealing with the human experience

Assessment

1. Teacher assessment of student journals

2. Teacher assessment of student mastery of vocabulary

3. Teacher assessment of student group work

4. Student self-assessment in journal commentary

5. Student peer assessment of group contributions (English highlights are presented in Figure 4–17)

FIGURE 4–17   English Highlights: Living in Other Cultures

Focus Points	Facts	Skills	Concepts
1. Understanding the use of English through study of another culture	1. The meanings of selected vocabulary words	1. Writing (various forms)	1. Understanding the relationship of a writer's perspective and culture
2. Developing an understanding of various forms of poetry	2. Rules and usage of parts and speech	2. Using a growing vocabulary	2. Understanding how language can be a cultural artifact
3. Increasing one's vocabulary	3. Terms associated with poetry	3. Using visual displays	3. The universality of literature and the human experience

Sample Activities:

1. Students will read two books and engage in a group study of the readings.

2. Students will research and write haiku.

3. Students will write essays and narratives.

COMMON LINKAGES

Materials

1. School-provided materials for research

2. Material provided in classroom activity

3. Student-generated material through classroom work

4. Additional material that relates to the theme

Activities and Time

1. In this one-day activity, students work at taking a small piece of information from an outside source and tripling it in size and scope with their own writing.

2. As students work toward developing a final product for a demonstration, they engage in research activities in each classroom geared toward a singular topic pertinent to the culture being investigated. This research would take place during the last three weeks of the unit, utilizing both class time and student homework. Teachers may wish to organize a form that helps students to stay on task and to budget time. Incorporated within this activity, teachers may wish to add a formal bibliography of resource information. Teachers may employ a second form enumerating organizational skills that will help both teachers and students to monitor progress.

3. The culmination presentation on the final day serves to showcase student products and demonstrate learning about another culture. It is designed to allow students to contribute, share with others, and produce a personal statement translating information gained through research and study into a original creation.

    The graphic organizers representing this unit are featured at the back of this section.

Skills

1. Cooperative and collaborative work skills

2. Positive social skills

3. Research skills

4. Elaborating and translating the products of study into a personal statement

5. Demonstrating

6. Organizing

7. Budgeting time

8. Linking study with personal experience

Concepts

1. The interdependence of the world community

2. The similarities found in separate cultures

3. Working collectively with the idea of a theme

4. The idea of diversity in a world community

5. The idea of diversity in a local community

Assessment

1. Teacher-generated checklist form for demonstration assessment by teacher

2. Teacher-generated checklist form for demonstration assessment by students

3. Teacher assessment of student progress through the research process

4. Student self-assessment in a written narrative

5. Teacher and student assessment of group work activities (interdisciplinary highlights are presented in Figure 4–18)

FIGURE 4–18   Interdisciplinary Activities: Living in Other Cultures

Interdisciplinary Objectives	Shared Skills	Shared Concepts
1. Connecting social studies and English learning	1. Developing collaborative and cooperative work skills	1. The interdependence of the world and school communities
2. Recognizing the similarities and diversity among various groups and national cultures	2. Organizing and presenting a demonstration	2. Working and understanding the idea of a theme
3. Developing an appreciation for being members of a world culture	3. Elaborating and translating the efforts of group and individual work into a final product	3. The diversity inherent in all cultures and in different cultures

Sample Activities:

1. Students will engage in individual and group activity as they conduct research toward developing a final product for presentation to the rest of the class.

2. Students will expand on small pieces of information and establish connections between separate pieces of information.

3. Students will present a final product in a setting in which all students share what they have learned.

SUMMARY

This unit is adaptable to a variety of topics and is adjustable in length to meet the needs of teachers and students. It brings students and teachers together in a common study and community activity. It can be expanded with the addition of individual activities for a day to a week. Units organized in this fashion provide a wealth of traditional knowledge and necessary skills for future study. Furthermore, these units inculcate in students a deeper understanding of the meaning of the material that is the focus of study.

This type of unit is particularly applicable to junior high school students. It provides the hands-on experiences and demonstrations that link class content with the understandings and intellectual constructions made by each student. In other words, through the use of two distinct subject areas, this unit invites students to become involved in their learning. Knowledge is not a random collection of isolated facts but has a purpose that is centered around a common theme. In this regard, the theme encourages interdisciplinary work and gives focus to both students and teachers.

In an era of global change in which mutual understandings are essential to survival, learning about another culture must include integrating the knowledge of a distinct global area with a sense of respect and admiration. This unit offers students the opportunity to do just that while at the same time mastering skills and discovering new factual material.

A Note about Resources and Materials

We estimate that the vast majority of junior high schools already have access to the material necessary to conduct a unit like this one. Because the library is the place to start, it means incorporating the school librarian as a partner in planning and conducting the unit. Additionally, even resource material that is dated, though not the best, is far better than nothing.

There is an enormous resource of videos on the educational market today, some of which are extremely well done. Many catalogues, particularly those dealing with video, offer a broad selection to meet the needs of most educators. Local libraries may also have video material that can be used to help teachers provide material for their students.

Social studies teachers usually have access to the resources necessary to begin a such a unit, since many already use a textbook. A textbook is useful at times to provide the skeleton on which the rest of learning can be built. If a teacher does not wish to use a text but opts to use more adequate material, then that is an excellent alternative. We also assume that social studies teachers have access to individual atlases that students can use throughout the year and not just for one short unit. Atlases are in themselves a wonderful hands-on and visual guide with which all children should become familiar.

The English teacher is confronted with a more complex problem regarding materials. Some materials from magazines and newspapers are accessible for both social studies and English through the library. Videotapes are available to buy or to rent. But most English teachers do not have a basic text to anchor the course that specializes in such a subject area.

In this unit, students were expected to read two books dealing with the cultural region under study. One book was to be read in the classroom. In this case, the teacher would need enough books to go around for all the students. If an entire grade is working on the same theme, the demands are magnified. Study three or four culture areas of the world, and the number of books needed skyrockets. The English teacher may need the help of department heads and administrators in locating additional resources for each student.

The second book students are expected to read poses an easier problem in terms of numbers. Again, if students are stumped about where to find a book, the school librarian is a key resource and is a person we have found always ready to help. Stories by authors such as Pearl Buck might be one resource, as would be works by other authors. Given the growing awareness of the importance of recognizing cultural contributions to the world community and celebration of diversity, there are greater numbers of appropriate books available for junior high school students. Again, even the most experienced teachers will benefit from using librarians as resources to help point them in the right direction.

As with other units, time can be an issue. For this unit to turn into a team teaching experience, schedule compromises must be made. Even for it to succeed as parallel teaming, time must be provided for designing a scope and sequence of skills and planning activities. Teachers need to decide on time issues in such a way as to maximize planning, teaming, and sharing resources. To achieve these goals, teachers need the assistance and support of administrators and schedulers.

This unit is flexible to encourage teachers to incorporate strategies designed by one, two, or more educators. These strategies should address issues related to involving student in their learning. Similarly, a set of criteria can be designed reflecting assessment of skill mastery and what strategies can be devised to ensure that all students meet acceptable levels of mastery.

This unit should serve as an example of what can be modified for a junior high school and for a senior high school. Units like this one, remind us that learning is not an activity limited to any one classroom, nor is it the province of a single teacher. It is broader in scope and a more inclusive process than we often wish to admit.

CHAPTER 5

Year-Long Themes

INTRODUCTION

"When all my teachers seem to be doing the same thing, it made it a lot easier for me and my friends to work together."

"Tom"

In earlier chapters we presented thematic interdisciplinary strategies that would give English and social studies teachers greater opportunities for collaborative work. Themes offer alternatives in the way we organize students and teachers in our schools. The short-term themes of Chapter 3 and the longer unit themes offered in Chapter 4 suggested strategies to focus teachers and students on common goals and outcomes. Themes provide the direction around which cooperative interdisciplinary strategies can be centered. The thematic models we offer encourage both *team teaching* situations among teachers and the parallel teaching that can foster *teaming* relationships. Consequently, themes are the focus points around which teaching and learning can take place.

In this chapter we suggest how individual or multiple themes can be used to focus a pair of classes, a grade, or an entire school around a common enterprise. In many ways, developing a year-long theme can be easier than creating an isolated unit or shorter activity. A year-long theme is more global and constantly demands the attention of teachers to designing activities. Year-long themes act as an umbrella; while they address a specific topic, they generate a wide number of opportunities for learning to occur.

This chapter also includes twenty titles, any one of which can be used as the centerpiece of an interdisciplinary theme study. Each title carries an annotated description of the topic and offers insights into teacher and school implementation. Also incorporated into the descriptions are examples of outcomes that the theme can generate in social studies and English classes as well as the larger school community.

TYPES OF THEMES

There are different types of year-long themes that educators can use. Taking a very broad view, we can group themes into three categories: skill-based, concept-based, or school and classroom community. Often, themes found in one of these areas will overlap and cross lines, while others remain distinct, though not mutually exclusive.

Skill-Based Themes

We have mentioned the idea of developing a *scope and sequence of skills* for each grade level throughout this book. Our efforts are not intended to be redundant. We feel the issue to be crucial in terms of answering questions about educational accountability and assessment. Teachers, working together within a cooperative setting and framework, should develop what they view as important *skills* for selected grade levels. Our point is that students at various grade levels should reach a mastery level of certain skills. Assessments of student mastery of skills should be made by individual teachers. These assessments deal with students at the individual level and are a constant source of feedback. A dialogue dealing with the accomplishments of a particular student is maintained through the cooperation of teachers, students, and parents.

This type of outcome can only occur with a concerted effort to develop a specific *scope and sequence of learning skills* by teachers working with specific populations. English and social studies teachers may not have the time to develop a complete scope and sequence, but they can make modifications and unofficially agree to highlight certain skills. This alternative offers a beginning step to linking two classrooms in an interdisciplinary activity dealing with skills.

The common ground shared by English and social studies classes is clear when one considers the learning skills taught in each subject area. These skills include completing specific tasks, such as building a web, to more general tasks, such as working productively as a member of a cooperative work group. In planning a year-long focus on skills, teachers need to identify the skills to be taught, when, and by whom. Goals and criteria need be established for determining mastery. Outcomes need to reflect individual student differences. The themes included in this section clearly identify for teachers carious grade-level-appropriate skills.

Concept-Based Themes

Earlier chapters suggested that teachers working in an interdisciplinary setting identify the concepts that are part of the lessons they design. This process can help teachers recognize which concepts are common to each subject area and which topics would provide the focus of a year-long exploration. Themes based on concepts provide a general framework for organizing interdisciplinary lessons.

Themes and the School Community

Throughout this book, we have presented thematic strategies which assist in creating interdisciplinary activity in schools. We firmly believe that teachers working together bring the most benefit to all students. We have also stressed that nontracked or mixed-ability classrooms in which cooperative work is stressed hold promise for students and teachers alike. Focusing on the issues raised by designing cooperative activities and setting student expectations can illustrate how themes addressing the interpersonal needs of a school community can be woven into an interdisciplinary curriculum. Topics for year-long study deal with community attitudes and behaviors. They offer opportunities for reflection and growth at the community level and within the individual. These themes must involve all members of the school community—teachers, students, and administrators—in an honest dialogue about who they are as people and what type of community they wish to share.

DESIGNING YEAR-LONG THEMATIC APPROACHES

By now, we expect to hear teachers asking with more than a little apprehension, "How do I start?" "What do I need to do?" "How much detail do I have to work through given the scope of the year?" "What will this do to my curriculum?" and "Where am I going to find the time to do this?"

Every one of those questions, and many others that we have heard or asked ourselves, are valid. The idea of a year's worth of programming is overwhelming. To think that an interdisciplinary and thematic curriculum can be designed and put into practice by English and social studies teachers on the spur of the moment is, in one sense, ludicrous and in another quite possible. Teachers and administrators need to think in terms of degree. There are ways of incorporating themes into an interdisciplinary curriculum that are feasible in a practical sense and respect the considerations of teachers facing change. Each approach offers a significant and realistic option for teachers to follow.

The Word for a Year

This approach to thematic interdisciplinary activity is linked to a theme about which English and social studies teachers might focus on during the course of a year. For example, the word *perspective* suggests that a common definition should be worked out by the teachers and then used on a regular basis within a social studies and an English class. Our experience with this type of activity identified the word *perspective* as *a way of looking at things*. Although this appears to be a simplistic definition, junior high school students readily identified with it. Consequently, the *concept* of a *perspective* was continually reinforced throughout the year and integrated into the curriculum. One important outcome of this theme was that junior high school students began to use the term *as it fits the definition constructed by the class*. Teachers could focus on the concept at their leisure without any more formal planning. Each discipline and the students taking the classes across the disciplines began to develop an understanding about the way each class was looking at elements of the world and what impacted their lives. Yet it was also interesting that a number of teachers continued to use the word *perspective* throughout the year. Perspective became a starting point and then served as a catalyst for the activities designed by English, social studies, science, and mathematics teachers.

Many words can serve to focus a school or a class. These words, which reflect how a community views itself or how groups focus and organize for academic inquiry, are powerful thematic teaching tools. Words such as *metamorphosis, diversity,* and *commitment* all have the ability to stimulate and sustain year-long interdisciplinary connections between classes. We offer twenty more annotated examples in this chapter.

Monthly Theme Meetings

This theme can become an integral component of life within a school community. The school, a grade, or English and social studies classes address an issue that is of concern to the school community. For example, topics such as *gender bias, racism, anti-Semitism,* or *civility* can be the focus point. English and social studies teachers address the theme individually through the activities that they structure with their students.

Once a month, or however often the educators working in a given community decide, the school community or that of a grade level would come together to explore the topic. Speakers may be brought in so faculty and students can experience additional points of view. Presentations can be made by members of the community as they view and address the issue. In each of these examples, the theme, agreed on by the teachers sharing a common population, becomes the nucleus of community-wide and interdisciplinary activity. While teachers would be encouraged to implement various *short-term strategies* or longer *interdisciplinary units,* classroom and curricular autonomy would be maintained.

This approach can fit in with other models, such as a *concept-based framework.* For example, the issues of war, revolution, or justice could serve to highlight a theme that brought students and teachers together on a regular basis. At the same time, these issues would be addressed within classes and still allow teachers to teach a subject-specific curriculum.

Year-Long Focused Interdisciplinary Work

At the highest level, there are themes that gain life from the shared subject matter of an English and a social studies class. It is commonality of focus and intent that gives them strength. In Chapter 4 we presented six units that are adaptable for building an interdisciplinary curriculum linked through units, semesters and years. Some of these activities require teachers to develop a *teaming* relationship and others a *team teaching* one. They all require that teachers have the opportunity to interact and work together.

PLANNING AND WORKING TOGETHER

These suggestions for topics and how to arrange year-long themes are meant to be flexible and to be modified by members of a school community to *meet their needs*. Central to our discussion is the recognition that teachers and students alike need the opportunity to work and plan together. Teachers will assume increased responsibility for providing a challenging educational environment that includes all learners. Teachers also will come to share responsibility with each other.

Administrators must become activists and offer teachers unlimited support. This is definitely true in terms of developing year-long themes. Whereas we see teachers as responsible for selecting a theme and designing classroom activities to support it, administrators, charged with the power of understanding and overseeing the organizational dynamics of a school, must energetically assist in making sure these efforts are put into practice. To observe passively or offer only tacit support will complicate and frustrate achieving the goals of a year-long interdisciplinary thematic study.

Year-Long Goals, Outcomes, and Assessment

Planning a year-long theme involves more than designing activities or arranging a schedule. Any year-long focus, whether as complex as a highly structured year of team teaching or as simple as parallel teaching linked by a common word or issue, needs to have a list of goals and desired outcomes. Teachers and students need to know where they are going on their intellectual journey. They need to have the direction provided by a clearly defined destination or, in this situation, the specific outcomes to be gained. These outcomes flow from developing a framework of interdisciplinary goals. Goals and outcomes for year-long thematic educational experiences do not need be contained in a fancy, lengthy, and polished statement. However, they do need to be clearly stated, understood, and accepted by everyone involved in the process.

Goals and planned outcomes need to reflect the individuality that students, as learners, bring to the classroom. It is this recognition of the diversity inherent in classrooms that gives strength to year-long themes. This strength is a further support for the learning experiences that take place under the thematic umbrella.

Assessment, though not as specific as one would find in short-term activities based on themes, is no less important. Once goals have been developed and outcomes established for students and faculty, assessment becomes an integral part of the thematic interdisciplinary program. Assessment not only should serve as a measure of particular issues such as skill mastery but also must reflect the impact on the student that would be generated by a year-long thematic interdisciplinary study.

SOME SUGGESTIONS FOR YEAR-LONG THEMATIC INTERDISCIPLINARY TOPICS

The remainder of this chapter highlights a sampling of topics we offer as year-long themes. Each supports the idea of interdisciplinary and heterogeneous activity. These themes provide focus points for students, teachers, and entire school communities. The following ideas might also be considered a starting point in reorganizing the traditional tracked school into an organization that is more responsive to the needs of those who make up the organization's community.

There are many more themes possible than these we now suggest. Any one of the themes we highlighted in Chapters 3 and 4 can be modified to work in a year-round setting and to serve as a broader base for structuring activity. In the same way, the themes we suggest as samples in the following section can be adapted to short- and long-term interdisciplinary units. We hope that educators use our suggestions as a model for building lists for their own schools.

Interdependence

This word can be used by an English and a social studies teacher to build a common ground during a year. Students would focus on the idea of interdependence and construct a definition that would be completed by year's end. This theme would allow for parallel teaching and would not seriously alter an existing curriculum. As an expanded interdisciplinary activity, it could serve as the basis for engaging students on a regular short-term or unit-length basis. This theme can be adapted for use in grades 7 through 12 and can form an additional basis for a thematic study by the school community.

Gender Studies

Gender offers a theme that can be tied directly into classroom instruction for both social studies and English teachers. Likewise, it can be adapted for use by a school community. Issues associated with gender, such as discrimination, equality, and stereotypes, are easily integrated into existing curricula. English and social studies teachers can parallel one another or use the time for short- or long-term study, such as the biography activity is highlighted in Chapter 3. As a large theme, it is appropriate for use in grades 7 through 12.

Fact versus Fiction

What is a fact? How are facts related to fiction? How do we determine what is a fact and what is not? These are some of the questions that help to focus attention the relationship of fact versus fiction. There are a great many more, a number limited only by what students can generate. This theme can be used in a parallel teaching situation or in various subthemes that direct concentrated interdisciplinary activity. The topic is well suited for use in the fields of English and social studies and can be adapted to any level of study at the junior and senior high school.

Skills

Learning skills make an excellent topic on which to focus the interdisciplinary activities of an English teacher and a social studies teacher. We have identified various skills, such as researching, writing narrative based on facts, and creating webs, which could become components of a master scope and sequence of skills geared to students at various grade levels. The scope and sequence becomes a theme teachers can use in organizing their lessons. Students and parents use the scope and sequence to help organize a framework of expectations. For example, a student in a grade level engaged in this type of activity would be presented an outline of what skills would be focused on an interdisciplinary nature. That student would be given a teacher-generated overview of why this activity was taking place and what it hoped to accomplish in terms of the individual student (goals and outcomes). Teachers would present when a skill would be introduced and then later reinforced. Mastery would focus on the accomplishments of the individual student (assessment) according to a set of teacher-generated criteria. In many ways, students would have a personal learning plan focusing on mastery of identifiable skills. In such a student-centered approach, competition between students is replaced by an individual student's personalized plan. This type of theme is easily adaptable to all junior and senior high school students. Our experience also has shown us that it is nonthreatening to students.

Perspective

We have used the year-long theme set by the word *perspective* (a way of looking at things, a way of presenting things) at the junior high school level. Perspective provided a very interesting sidelight to what was taking place in various classes. For example, perspective was seen as carrying a number of related meanings as students worked toward a common definition that could be applied in an interdisciplinary setting. The theme went on for the year and found its way into many separate units. Again, the focus was constant, yet much of the interdisciplinary activity consisted of teachers using the same word in separate classes. Perspective can also be applied to a school community as students and teachers look at the focus of their own community and at the many individual perspectives that exist within the population.

The Struggle between Freedom and Control

For a senior high school class, this conflict can be a valuable link between their English class and their social studies class. The conflict between these two elements of social life fits within much of the literature read by high school students. It also represents a theme common in history and in related social studies courses. Teachers working in parallel situations focusing on this topic will find that common linkages will occur and provide avenues for further and closer interdisciplinary activity. The struggle between freedom and control is also a theme that can be expanded to include the school community. It can provide the basis of a self-study that deals with the tensions produced as groups of people struggle to find a balance point for their differences.

Compromise

This theme represents a start for a community self-assessment. It can lead to discovering various methods for dealing with differences. Compromise makes all members of a community reflect on their own behavior and actions in terms of others. It also is a theme that is applicable in both social studies and English classes. This theme deals with issues addressed in content areas and provides openings for other related interdisciplinary thematic work. The role and meaning of compromise can lead into an activity exploring issues, principles, and conflict. Although compromise is applicable to both junior and senior high school levels, it is particularly appropriate for use in high schools.

Family

Family is a constant theme in the content of both English and social studies classes. The power and impact of family membership is important to understanding who we are as individuals and as members of a community. The roles dictated by family membership and the portrayal of these roles in fiction and in historical situations provide additional areas for study. Family can be the focus in both junior and senior high school classes. this theme offers the opportunity for parallel study and for team teaching.

The Test

We as a people deal with being tested. This is true in the way we represent our lives through fiction as well as in the drama that historically frames our collective experience. Students can identify with a test in the traditional sense of schooling. This theme encourages students to make the leap and see how they are being tested during the school year. The theme is well suited for senior high school students. It offers opportunities to understand the demands that spring from a social existence. It can lead to interdisciplinary activity geared toward viewing the tests we all face or to other themes related to daily living. This theme involves students and teachers in their learning because it grounds what is learned in the classroom with the experiences of everyday life.

Cause and Effect

This theme representing a relationship forms the basis for understanding who we are and what we do. It is applicable to any grade in junior or senior high schools. Cause and effect is clearly not limited to specific disciplines but can easily be applied to the course content found in social studies and English classes. In the same way that cause and effect fits thematically within the curriculum of a course, it also provides an option for interdisciplinary applications between the two disciplines. In many ways, as the connections become more and more apparent, cause and effect is not limited to a study from a united English and social studies perspective. It can also focus a school community's attempt to understand the relationships within the experience of participatory community membership.

Order versus Chaos

We have used this year-long theme as a way of establishing a continuum on which students continually examine where varying societies, including their own, are located in this struggle. As a teaching strategy in social studies, it provides a graphic and specific way of identifying tension and struggle as people have moved from one area to the next. However, it offers many opportunities for parallel links between English and social studies. It can begin as a study as basic as creating and understanding the need for an orderly classroom and move on to the issues of nations struggling with law enforcement and people contending with personal issues. Additionally, there are a number of interdisciplinary links that can be expanded into strategies lasting over a period of weeks.

Diversity

Diversity is a theme that in many ways cannot be separated and maintained as subject-specific. By its very nature it needs to be examined from multiple viewpoints. Issues dealing with diversity such as culture, heritage, ethnicity, gender studies, and a multitude of other possibilities, offer many opportunities for year-long study encompassing the entire school community. The topic is especially well suited for English and social studies classes. The wealth of literature with diversity as a theme is abundant. In social studies classes, diversity is a continuing issue with which most societies and civilizations have struggled. Additionally, the topic easily lends itself to study in a grade level from junior to senior high school.

Love

With a secondary school population, a study of themes cannot overlook love. Although young people in each generation may think they have discovered love, the universality of the concept alone makes it worth studying. It is an excellent and involving theme for parallel study in high school English and social studies classes. There are many possible interdisciplinary strategies for paralleling and joining classes to study the nature and impact of love on various societies throughout history. A number of possibilities also exist for involving other areas such as health classes, science classes, and daily living courses. This theme also offers a number of ways to develop the skill of comparing and contrasting, which we have emphasized as so important, as students examine the changes in expressions and practices of love over the centuries.

Choice

Choice is not only a theme but also a life skill. However, it is one that is often overlooked or given only cursory attention. Yet since students will have to live with the consequences of many choices that they will make now and in the future, they must understand the concept of choice as well as learn how to make sound and justifiable decisions. As a result, this is an area that certainly can be emphasized at any grade level. An excellent way of paralleling this theme is through activities such the "Who Am I's," highlighted earlier, and biography studies. As students analyze personal and societal choices through their English and social studies classes, the concept takes on life and easily transfers into activities that place students in various choice making situations.

Values

What are values? What is the difference between personal, family, societal, and governmental values? What happens when personal values come into conflict with societal values? Are there universal values that form a code of conduct by which to live? These are all issues that our students grapple with daily as they struggle to gain personal definition. Therefore, this is a theme that by its very personal nature can take advantage of students' past history, experience, and knowledge and use these areas to involve students in a structured analysis and definition of this abstract concept. English and social studies abound with examples of human beings' struggle to determine value. By its very nature, this theme can be easily paralleled by teachers who coordinate certain activities that stress this theme. Additionally, since all courses have value within what they teach and prioritize, broad strokes are easily drawn that encompass the full curricula of the school.

Survival

Again, this is a theme that is already on students' minds. They are learning to survive school, heartaches, defeats, victories, love, divorce, neighborhoods, fears, and joys. Although as teachers we tend to look at survival as dealing with the larger issues of war, famine, or societal upheaval, our students are attempting to survive growing up. As a result of this direct applicability to the lives of our client population, we should address this issue as a common theme between our classes and answer concerns that are student-oriented on this theme. As with the other themes, there are a multitude of ways to make connections between English and social studies. This type of theme is especially powerful, as students can be the source of the topics for the study. If students identify the areas of survival about which they are concerned, while the school meets this need by paralleling the issues in English and social studies activities, very powerful learning will occur.

The Quest

This is a theme as common as the existence of the school and as old as human beings. From the time they board the bus or begin the walk to school, to asking a question in class or asking a person for a date on Friday night, students are following a quest. They are in pursuit of something. They are on a metaphoric journey that will take them somewhere. As teachers, we must give definition to their trip. Through paralleling and teaming, we can support students on the expedition as we emphasize the importance of recognizing the quest as a theme that is universal in history and language arts. This theme offers teachers the ability again to use knowledge students already have developed and to enlarge that knowledge through further study and identification. Instead of waiting until graduation to tell them they are on a journey, we need to focus early on the concept as we help them read and interpret the map.

Relationships

By its very definition, this theme should be studied in all classes, not merely English and social studies. As we attempt to develop students' abilities to recognize relationships, we must model relationships ourselves through our interactions as teachers and making connections to each other's disciplines. As students learn to see relationships through our supporting this concept, they are developing hierarchal skills of recognition, clarification, and classification. Merely paralleling what is going on in different classes will emphasize the importance of identifying and creating relationships. This is also an important theme for teachers, as it keeps them thinking of the big picture and not departmentalizing everything to the point that each concept exists in isolation. It is also an appropriate theme for all classes from grades 7 to 12.

Goals

What are goals? Do we have goals as teachers that are clearly identified to students? Do we ask students what their goals are for our classes? Do we create a series of common goals to achieve together during the course of our shared time? Does society develop goals that move it along a certain course? These are questions that add definition to the theme. As a theme, goals are again an area that is very personal and begins with the student and the knowledge, ambition, and feelings that each one brings to our classes. therefore, if we make this a common theme in English and social studies, we can parallel individual and group goals in subject-specific areas to the literature and development of civilization. As these three components come together, students will make the connections between personal goals and the directions that influence a society. As with other themes, this concept is equally adaptable for all disciplines that parallel each other through repetition of sharing, creating, and meeting goals as a community.

Rights and Responsibilities

This is a theme around which English and social studies teachers can easily build a common ground for a year-long focus. Students would focus on defining rights and constructing a definition of rights that would evolve throughout the year's study. Through paralleling and interdisciplinary work, students would gradually learn to appreciate the complexity of the word *rights*. As the definition evolved through the two courses, students would learn that rights have a very different meaning than *license* or *unbridled freedom*. Through an evolving view of rights, students would struggle with *responsibilities* and discover a cause-and-effect relationship. Additionally, this theme easily lends itself to a community study as a school functions through certain rights and responsibilities. It is only by having students put these ideas together rather than separate them that school becomes a community in more than *term*, but in a definition of a group of people coming together for a common and mutually understood series of goals and values as they pursue knowledge.

CHAPTER 6

Conclusion

INTRODUCTION

> *"I remember best when the social studies and the math teacher brought our classes together in junior high school. We had two teachers help us make kites."*
>
> "Jeremy"

This book has suggested alternatives for educators to follow as they build schools that provide the highest levels of educational experience for all students. These schools are not structured by arbitrary criteria such as student tracks or departmental lines but are open to the processes of sharing knowledge. Such schools benefit both students and teachers by setting high expectations and utilizing the strengths that teachers and students carry into the learning environment of a classroom.

We are teachers who see the need for this type of change in our schools. We recognize the meanings that are advocated by various theorists and the results that have been demonstrated by the research. At the same time, we are aware of the needs voiced by teachers and administrators as they cope with change.

HETEROGENEITY IN CLASSROOMS

> *"I think putting everyone together, regardless of their level, is good because, I mean, you're always helping each other. I learn a lot by helping to teach other people and being taught by other people."*
>
> "Sherm"

Schools that focus on organizational structures drawn along traditional bureaucratic lines will not fit the needs of educators in the next century. As educators having worked in both tracked and nontracked schools, we understand the need to recognize and value the individuality of all students. Schools are communities in which we need to bring people together to develop the contributions offered by the uniqueness and diversity of the population of those communities. The activities we have presented in this book capitalize on the solutions and contributions that are possible in mixed-ability classrooms. These activities represent and utilize the diversity and potential within all schools.

INITIATING CONNECTIONS

Our efforts, grounded in the experience of teachers and administrators, have offered some ways of connecting educational theory to the practitioners in the classroom. These strategies reflect the current concerns and literature about adapting schools to meet the needs of the next century and a culturally diverse society. Yet our suggestions only constitute a beginning. Teachers, as well as students, should have the freedom to create and re-create their classroom work rather than simply following the arbitrary outline dictated by others. Our strategies celebrate the possibilities of what teachers and students can achieve by working together in schools that are organized to enable this collaboration. We strongly believe that the hope and promise of public schools is dependent on connecting theory and practice to students' needs.

The ideas incorporated in this book represent a continuation of our efforts to help educators adapt to changing schools and society (presented in Nowicki & Meehan, 1996). That book, focused on social studies classrooms, suggests methods that enable teachers and students to gain control of the learning environment and processes in their classrooms. Linking interdisciplinary strategies across a school, as we propose in this book, allows a school community to take control of the direction of its learning. Not only should students and teachers work together, but teachers must share professional experience and knowledge. Schools must become collegial places where ideas are exchanged. Our assumptions further reflect our belief that schools must become places of learning dedicated to meeting the needs of the future. Strategies need to be developed that allow students to take meaning from their experiences and translate these meanings into demonstrated learning products.

The suggestions in this book relate directly to creating cooperative activities for both students and teachers. We believe these strategies answer many of the arguments of schools fighting change and provide alternatives to those attempting to restructure classrooms. However, administrators must provide effective inservice training and time for teachers to work together to develop classroom strategies and models.

We are offering a synthesis in which the roles of students and teachers interact and cross traditional and organizationally shaped boundaries through interdisciplinary work. This type of activity enables teachers to create a more optimal learning situation in which students and teachers, working together, develop a broader base of knowledge. It also requires the school, as a community, to rethink the frames of organization that have traditionally served to arrange teacher and student lives.

ASSESSMENT

"I think that I could have covered more mate-
rial in some classes, but I don't think that I
would have known the material as well as I
do. It's like I would've been able to say some-
thing looks right but now I can say it is right."

"Becca"

Our experience in teaching mixed-ability classes has reminded us of the
importance of the individual as well as the group. Our emphasis is on
creating a learning situation that is not dependent on the ideal of sorting
students along the lines of arbitrarily set criteria. These situations ultimately require that students work against each other rather with each
other. Unfortunately, the negative effects of sorting frequently contribute
to the high dropout rates in schools where all students do not benefit
equally from the learning experience. We believe all students can achieve
in schools that foster the connections to involve all students in their classroom work and in the greater purpose of schooling. Interdisciplinary efforts based on themes assist educators in creating these learning situations.

In terms of assessment, students are responsible for meeting standards and expectations set by students and teachers. As we have suggested earlier in this book, assessment is not simply a valuative experience. It is an opportunity to reflect on an individual's progress in specific
areas and to develop a plan that is geared to a particular student. Assessment is not a punitive activity but one that contributes to intellectual
growth and learning skills development.

Each of the strategies presented in this book contains an assessment
component. We have left these modules flexible enough to encourage teachers to personalize what they develop for assessment. Very often we include the idea of peer assessment because, as stated earlier, learning is
not simply an individual activity; it involves others in a collaborative exchange of information and ideas. Assessment strategies geared toward
developing individual strengths need to include the feedback of peers,
self-reflection, and teacher input.

Accountability and Responsibility

Our focus on promoting the achievement and growth of the individual
does not negate the importance of individual accountability and responsibility on the part of students. This book has presented a number of work-
able options that enable students to accept responsibility and to hold themselves accountable for their efforts and final products. Students should
not simply be consumers of educational experiences presented by others,
nor should they be merely entertained and occupied by teachers. Our suggestions for thematic interdisciplinary connections across curricula and
within the school clearly involve students in the process of education. If
schools are to be effective in meeting the demands of the next century,
they need to include students as contributing members of a school community and as participants in their own learning. If this is to take place,

students, like administrators and teachers, should be held accountable and responsible for their efforts in the daily life of school communities.

Assessment is integral in establishing the necessary accountability and responsibility. It must deal with clear expectations and cover many areas of student learning. Students need to know the expectations as well as learning to identify their own strengths and weaknesses. They need constant feedback from teachers and from peers. They need the sense of involvement that allows them to reflect on their own efforts and experience. If students are to be functional as the adults of the next century, they need the skill of self-assessment.

ANXIOUS VOICES

Some are not yet ready to embrace the concepts and themes underlying our work. Other teachers with administrative support and encouragement, will commit the time and energy to adapting classes and curricula toward the ideal of heterogeneity. Our experience also suggests that there are others willing to try a small piece of work dedicated to creating interdisciplinary lines. Administrators and teachers need to seize that small piece of work as a starting point: Create a short-term interdisciplinary activity. Discuss the possibilities of year-long themes. Rethink a school schedule. Dare to look at ways of organizing teachers and students that will address the needs of a culturally diverse and technologically literate society. Identify the needs of each student. Focus on involving students in their learning. Clearly, options are essential. Educators and students need the freedom to learn, explore, and create. They need to build their learning and professional experiences in ways that are open to change in practice and in theory.

Creating Student Realities

Interdisciplinary activity should allow students to re-create knowledge. They should become owners of what their work produces. They construct the connections that come from their studies. The strategies in this book place students in the central spot of education. It holds them accountable and responsible for being involved in the activities that lead to the acquisition of knowledge.

Students face a myriad of distractions from the larger society. In some communities, violence in homes, schools, and neighborhoods represents a major problem. In others, too many students are attuned to the passive entertainment offered by electronic media and games. In still other communities, poverty and its resulting obstacles force students to deal with issues of far more immediate concern than classrooms from which they feel alienated.

Classrooms and schools need to become places where students are vested with a level of control and ownership. Classrooms need to be places where students develop a level of self-interest in their learning and of acquiring knowledge. Teachers need to have a hook that grabs students' attention and involves them in the experience of learning and in making positive contributions to the school community.

Teachers

If schools are to be places where students are enabled to learn and to create their knowledge in a sense of true ownership, then teachers must be allowed to do the same with their teaching. Teachers also need a sense of ownership. They need to be able to develop curriculum and design activities to involve their students. Limiting teachers' ability to design and develop curriculum will seriously impede the implementation of interdisciplinary strategies. Ultimately, teachers need the freedom and support to be professionals.

Teachers required to teach a curriculum that has no flexibility and does not allow for individual creativity are in the same position as disenfranchised students. There are other institutional constraints with which teachers must struggle, such as standardized tests or college requirements. Yet these constraints should be flexible enough to allow teachers to develop individual interpretations of curriculum and teaching.

Teachers, like students, need to be held accountable and responsible for what goes on in a classroom. Student-centered and activity-based classrooms are not an excuse for abdicating responsibility for what happens in these classrooms. A student-centered environment places many demands on the teacher's time within a class period. Sufficient planning must be made to address the activities, the presentation of the material, the acquisition of material, and the final assessment. In this type of classroom, teachers use the curriculum in ways that encourage students to develop a sense of creativity and ownership. Teachers become educational leaders when they have the freedom that comes with accepting professional responsibility—the freedom to teach.

Administrators

School administrators are primary components of the teaching/learning process. The principal is the single most important person within the school. This is the person who is responsible for establishing the environment, the attitude, the support, and the encouragement within that building. Administrators need to be true partners in encouraging and fostering the processes of rethinking the structures of the school. For teachers and students to do what they do best, administrators need to provide the environment in which connecting activities such as thematic interdisciplinary education a reality, administrators and especially principals need to take an activist role that enables teachers and students to make classrooms open and creative places in all schools.

Schools as Organizations

Schools can and should be places where all students can develop and exchange ideas. Students, teachers, and administrators should not be separated by arbitrary barriers established by organizations intent on self-preservation. Recreating schools to foster interdisciplinary activity is a challenge to the existence of antiquated organizational structures dedicated to managing and categorizing teachers, students, and administrators. The administrators who are responsible for overseeing the organization of schools must recognize better ways of meeting the needs of a diverse and demanding society. They must experiment with flexible schedules, hours, allocation of teachers, and cross-disciplinary activity.

The Need to Recognize the Contributions of Others

Interdisciplinary activities thrive on the efforts and contributions of teachers and in the efforts and products of students. Creating the atmosphere, culture, and daily organizational environment that promotes successful and creative interaction among community members is often the province of administrators. We propose that the three groups work together. Every teacher, student, and administrator must recognize what others have to offer for the improvement of the school community. This is true not only in the way administrators, students, and teachers need to view each other but also in how they perceive and deal with their peers.

Cooperative Classroom Work

The interdisciplinary approaches based on thematic inquiry include our belief in the cooperative classroom. As with issues such as heterogeneous grouping, creating environments in which students construct a personal knowledge, or developing interdisciplinary links based on themes, our positions are based in the professional literature and, most important, in our own classroom experiences. While there are no panaceas, cooperative work, an interdisciplinary school, heterogeneous classrooms, and empowered teachers who are educational leaders within the organization of a school are all important. These educational components can make significant improvements in how schools prepare students for membership in society. The process of collective problem solving can enable the students of today to expand their individual potential while participating in group tasks.

Creating Collaborative Schools

The desire and opportunity to work together are not enough to create bridges across the organizational divisions that exist within schools. Every member of the school community first needs to recognize the potential for improvement offered by other members. This demands a level of trust and respect for others from all community members. Interdisciplinary learning experiences can create the small yet essential bridges needed at the student-to-student or teacher-to-teacher level. Small bridges within a community form a grassroots strength that fosters the sense of a community that a school needs to thrive. Schools must focus on instilling the value and importance of community rather than fomenting division through separating and categorizing educators and students.

TOWARD BETTER AND MORE RESPONSIVE SCHOOLS

As teachers, we see a need to creating better schools as a part of the process of life. This is part of what we are. Those in the teaching profession try to influence and improve the lives of those we teach. In many ways, teaching is a noble and an enabling profession. We want to leave the world and society a better place.

The struggle of society and human experience has for the most part been toward bettering the conditions of those in societies that follow. There are times in history when self-gain becomes the preeminent concern and side trips regressing into very unproductive human experiences occur. But in the long term of human experience, it has been the quiet yet overwhelming drive to improve what currently exists that has been the center and spark of change. Schools, particularly in the growing world community fostered by the technological revolution of the past two centuries, are at the forefront of change. They need to be places where alternatives are explored. Schools also need to be places where differences are worked out while still enabling the individual to develop.

Interdisciplinary Activity through Themes

To effect change, communities often need a vehicle. For middle, junior, and senior high schools, interdisciplinary activity offers such an opportunity. It links teachers and students in a process that is focused on what is contained in the curriculum. Interdisciplinary activities can alter a curriculum. We have offered a selection of strategies that can be adapted to what already exists. The model we suggest can easily be adopted by school communities interested in refocusing the process of learning. We see themes as a primary means for arranging strategies that link school populations in a common purpose.

Other Disciplines and Reconfigured Schools

Although this book has dealt with the connections between social studies and English classes, there are many other alternatives to creating interdisciplinary activity. We chose English and social studies because we saw the connections. We have both worked in linking social studies and English with mathematics and science classes as well as with languages, home economics, and industrial arts. Whenever teachers have been willing to work together, we have capitalized on the opportunity.

We have both been frustrated at times by schedules and by administrative action. We have worked in rigidly structured schools where teacher interaction and student interaction were stifled. Yet we have also seen the enormous opportunities offered by bringing teachers together around common themes and commonalities as students are encouraged to construct their learning. We realize that interdisciplinary connections must be made among all departments in schools striving to build lively and supportive intellectual communities.

SOME FINAL THOUGHTS

We end this book as we began it. In our view, schools are still vibrant places filled with enormous potential. They are our society's link to the future. Both of us have felt that schools spend too much time reacting to events around them rather than being proactive places where the future is truly shaped. As teachers, we have felt the professional frustration of working in unresponsive organizations that demanded that students and teachers fit as if they were line items in a budget.

We have listened to complaints from parents and students about unresponsive schools. In our opinion, some of those complaints are justified, but others are not. While teachers and administrators should ensure that schools are responsive places, students and parents need to ensure that students accept the accountability and the responsibility that comes from creating schools as interconnected communities.

We both recognize that there are enormous societal issues reflecting complex social, economic, and political problems that tear at the heart of school communities. The issues of violence and drugs in schools will not be easily addressed. The frustration of those students and teachers who lead lives of quiet desperation and survival needs to be addressed. However, we do hope that our suggestions will stimulate improvement and create a positive difference in the lives of teachers and students.

"We still could be better."
"Jude"

Bibliography

Armstrong, T. (1994). *Multiple intelligences.* Alexandria, VA: Association for Supervision and Curriculum Development.

Barth, R. S. (1988). *School: A community of leaders: Building a professional culture in schools* (Ann Lieberman, ed.). New York: Teachers College Press.

Barth, R. S. (1990). *Improving schools from within.* San Francisco: Jossey-Bass.

Becker, H. S., Geer, B., Hughes, E. C., & Strauss, A. L. (1984). *Boys in white.* New Brunswick, NJ: Transaction Books.

Bereiter, C., & Scardamalia, M. (1987). *The psychology of written composition.* Hillsdale, NJ: Lawrence Erlbaum Associates.

Blase, J., & Kirby, P. C. (1992). *Bringing out the best in teachers: What effective principals do.* Newbury Park, CA: Corwin Press.

Bolman, L. G., & Deal, T. E. (1988). *Modern approaches to understanding and managing organizations.* San Francisco: Jossey-Bass.

Bolman, L. G., & Deal, T. E. (1991). *Reframing organizations: Artistry, choice and leadership.* San Francisco: Jossey-Bass.

Bolman, L. G., & Deal, T. E. (1994). *Becoming a teacher leader: From isolation to collaboration.* Thousand Oaks, CA: Corwin Press.

Boone, R. S. (1992). *Literature and language.* Evanston, IL: McDougal, Littell.

Bowles, S., & Gintis, H. (1976). *Schooling in capitalist America.* New York: Basic Books.

Brandvik, M. L. (1990). *Writing process activities kit: Seventy-five ready-to-use lessons and worksheets for grades 7–12.* West Nyack, NY: Center for Applied Research in Education.

Brubaker, J. W., Case, C. W., & Reagan, T. G. (1994). *Becoming a reflective educator: How to build a culture of inquiry in the schools.* Thousand Oaks, CA: Corwin Press.

Caine, R. N., & Caine, G. (1991). *Making connections: Teaching and the human brain.* Alexandria, VA: Association for Supervision and Curriculum Development.

Charon, J. (1989). *Symbolic interactionism,* 3rd ed. Englewood Cliffs, NJ: Prentice-Hall.

Corbett, H. D., Firestone, W. A., & Rossman, G. B. (1987). Resistance to planned change and the sacred in school cultures. *Educational Administration Quarterly, 23*(4).

Elbow, P. (1981). *Writing with power.* New York: Oxford University Press.

Elbow, P. (1986). *Embracing contraries: Explorations in learning and teaching.* New York: Oxford University Press.

Elbow, P. (1990). *What is English?* New York: Modern Language Association.

Elbow, P., & Blau, S. (1992). *The writer's craft: Idea to expression.* Evanston, IL: McDougal, Littell.

Evans, D. L. (1991, March). The realities of untracking a high school, *Educational Leadership, 48*(6).

Fullan, M. (1992). *The new meaning of educational change.* New York: Teachers College Press.

Gardner, H. (1989). *To open minds.* New York: Basic Books.

Goodlad, J. (1984). *A place called school.* New York: McGraw-Hill.

Goodson, F. T. (1994, September). Reading and writing across genres: Textual form and social action in the high school. *Journal of Reading, 38*(1), 6–12.

Greenlaw, M. J., Shepperson, G. M., & Nistler, R. (1992, March). A literature approach to teaching about the middle ages. *Language Arts, 69,* 200–204.

Griffin, G. A. (1990). *Leadership for curriculum improvement: The school administrator's role in school's as collaborative cultures—Creating the future now* (Ann Lieberman, ed.). London: Falmer Press.

Joyce, B., & Weil, M. (1972). *Models of Teaching.* Englewood Cliffs, NJ: Prentice-Hall.

Kirby, D., Liner, T., & Vinz, R. (1988). *Inside out: Developmental strategies for teaching writing.* Portsmouth: Boynton/Cook/Heinemann.

Kohn, A. (1993). *Punished by rewards: The trouble with gold stars, incentive plans, A's, praise, and other bribes.* Boston: Houghton Mifflin.

Lazear, D. (1991a). *Seven ways of knowing: Teaching for multiple intelligences.* Palatine, IL: Skylight Publishing.

Lester, J. (1969). *Black folktales.* New York: Grove Press.

Lieberman, A. (1988). *Building a professional culture in schools.* New York: Teachers College Press.

Lieberman, A., & Miller, L. (1991). "Revisiting the social realities of teaching." In A. Lieberman & L. Miller (Eds.), *Staff development for education in the '90's.* New York: Teachers College Press.

Little, J. W. (1990). Teachers as colleagues. In A. Lieberman (Ed.), *Schools as collaborative cultures: Creating the future now.* London: Falmer Press.

Muschla, G. R. (1991). *The writing teacher's book of lists with ready-to-use activities and worksheets.* Englewood Cliffs, NJ: Prentice-Hall.

Noll, E. (1994, October). Social issues and literature circles with adolescents. *Journal of Reading, 38*(2), 88–93.

Nowicki, J. J. (1992). *A school as a crucible of change: A case study of restructuring and a faculty's culture.* Ph.D. dissertation, University of Massachusetts at Amherst, Amherst, Massachusetts.

Nowicki, J. J. (1993, April 29). *Students respond to detracking: A small scale study.* Paper presented at the New England Educational Research Education Annual Meeting, Portsmouth, New Hampshire.

Nowicki, J. J. (1994). *Multiple perspectives in program design and implementation: School policy and "at risk" learners.* Paper presented at the New England Educational Research Organization annual meetings, Rockport, Maine.

Nowicki, J. J., & Felton, L. (1991, Spring). Students respond to detracking: A small scale study. *Pioneer Practitioner, 21*(1), 22–24.

Nowicki, J. J., & Meehan, K. F. (1996). *The collaborative social studies class: A resource for teachers, grades 7 through 12.* Boston: Allyn and Bacon.

Oakes, J. (1985). *Keeping track: How schools structure inequality.* New Haven: Yale University Press.

Orwell, G. (1949). *1984.* New York: Harcourt, Brace Jovanovich.

Page, R. N. (1991). *Lower-track classrooms: A curricular and cultural perspective.* New York: Teachers College Press.

Pinciss, G. M., et al. (1985). *Exploring in the arts.* New York: Holt, Rinehart and Winston.

Rossman, G. B., Corbett, H. D., & Firestone, W. A. (1988). *Change and effectiveness in schools: A cultural perspective.* Albany: SUNY Press.

Ryder, R. J. (1994). Using frames to promote critical writing. *Journal of Reading, 38*(3), 210–218.

Rylant, C. (1993). *I had seen castles.* New York: Harcourt, Brace.

Shakespeare, W. (1952). *The complete works* (G. B. Harrison, Ed.). New York: Harcourt, Brace & World.

Shibutani, T. (1955). Reference groups as perspectives. *The American Journal of Sociology.* Cited in J. Charon, (1989), *Symbolic interactionism,* 3rd ed. Englewood Cliffs, NJ: Prentice-Hall.

Simpson, A. (1994, December–January). Not the class novel: A different reading program. *Journal of Reading, 38*(4), 290–294.

Waller, W. (1932). *The sociology of teaching.* New York: Wiley.

Weber, M. (1946). Characteristics of bureaucracy. *Sociological theory: A book of readings,* 3rd ed. (L. A. Coser & B. Rosen, Eds.) (1957). London: Macmillan.

Weber, M. (1947). *The theory of social and economic organization.* (T. Parsons, Trans.). New York: Oxford University Press.

Weber, M. (1956). Some consequences of bureaucratization. *Sociological theory: A book of readings,* 3rd ed. (L. A. Coser, & B. Rosen, Eds.) (1957). London: Macmillan.

Wheelock, A. (1992). *Crossing the tracks.* New York: The New Press.

Index

Verse:
 communicating through, 42–44
 logic of creating, 42
 as source of information, 42–44
 use of to communicate a coherent thought, 42
Videotapes, creation and use of, 49, 97–99, 104–106, 125, 127, 133, 135, 141, 151, 168, 175
Visual learners, use of graphic organizers with, 51

Waller, W., 3
War:
 causes of, 126
 issues of, 86–89
 societal impact of, 121–130
Weber, M., 3
Webs, as form of graphic organizer, 51–53
Weil, M., 133
Wheelock, A., 5, 7, 20, 22
Women, contributions of, 60–62
Working together:
 by students, importance of, 6–7
 by teachers, importance of, 4–6, 7
 as a tradition in other spheres, 24
World Cultures (*see also* Social Studies)
 short-term themes for, 69–71
World Geography (*see also* Social Studies)
 short-term themes for, 69–71
World History, short-term themes for, 42–44, 48–50, 54–56, 60–62, 66–68, 69–71, 72–75, 76–78, 86–89
World Studies, short-term themes for, 83–85, 90–92, 97–99, 100–102, 103–106
World War I:

as cause of World War II, 121–130
causes of, 121–130
effects of, 121
Europe during, map of, 122
scope and sequence for, 31
Writers, effective, development of, 10
Writing skills, at the ninth-grade level, 12
Writing, descriptive, 63–65

Year-long interdisciplinary themes, 177–196
 concept-based, 178
Year-long themes, listed:
 cause and effect, 184
 choice, 185
 compromise, 184
 diversity, 185
 fact versus fiction, 182
 family, 184
 freedom and control, struggle between, 183
 gender studies, 182
 goals, 181
 interdependence, 182
 learning skills, 183
 love, 185
 order vs. chaos, 185
 perspective, 183
 the quest, 186
 relationships, 187
 rights and responsibilities, 188
 skills, 183
 survival, 186
 the test, 184
 values, 186